CITIZENS AS SOVEREIGNS

Citizens
as Sovereigns

Paul H. Appleby

Foreword by W. Averell Harriman

SYRACUSE UNIVERSITY PRESS 1962

For Dave and Andy
Tom and Jim
Paul, Ruth, and Karen

Contents

vii

Foreword

FEW men are more highly qualified than Paul
Appleby to discuss the role of citizens in our democratic government, not only on a national, but on a state and local level as
well. As a private citizen, born in Missouri, he has lived in a
number of states, in a score of communities, large and small, in
the Middle West, the South, and on both coasts. He started his
career in the traditional manner of the truly successful business-
man—as a newsboy.

As a publisher and editor of several newspapers, he saw the
many sides of American life.

As an educator, he brought new understanding to old problems.

The most conservative Chamber of Commerce member would
respect him for having met a payroll.

With this varied background, he made an unusual contribution within government itself. He served two Presidents as
intimate adviser; and as the right arm of a Governor of New York
State he brought fresh appreciation of the responsibilities of
state government.

In each of his many positions he gained insight into what the
varied needs of people for government are and how government
could serve them.

His first experience in the federal government was with the Department of Agriculture, at the height of the Depression, when he saw the plight of farmers turning desperately to their government to save them from disaster. He became familiar with all aspects of the federal government in the Bureau of the Budget under both President Roosevelt and President Truman.

Paul Appleby firmly believes in Abraham Lincoln's philosophy of government, epitomized in these two statements:

> "The legitimate object of government, is to do for a community of people, whatever they need to have done, but cannot do, *at all*, or cannot, *so well do*, for themselves—in their separate, and individual capacities."
>
> "In all that the people can individually do as well for themselves, government ought not to interfere."

I can speak with some authority about Paul Appleby. Our paths have crossed frequently over the past thirty years—not only in this country but in wartime London as well. Our most intimate association was during the period he served as Budget Director while I was Governor of New York.

I had learned from my experience in Washington to use the Bureau of the Budget as a means of controlling the activities of all departments of the government, both in stimulating imaginative ideas and in routing out extravagance and incompetence. A Budget Director is proverbially the "evil spirit" in an organization, but not so Appleby. He won the respect and affection of those he dealt with—even the Chairmen of the Appropriations Committees, and in a Republican-controlled state legislature that is no mean achievement. Although I have not had recent occasion to consult them, I make this statement without the slightest fear of contradiction. I must confess that I would hesitate to speak so confidently on many subjects.

Paul Appleby learned to appreciate the need for weighing political, as well as administrative, factors in reaching decisions. Without a proper balance, success in government cannot be achieved. He understood that "political" decisions are really

basic policy decisions. While dean of the Maxwell Graduate
School of Citizenship and Public Affairs of Syracuse University
he made a unique contribution to the study of government. He
opposed the long-held theory that administration could be developed as a science, independent of policy, and pioneered the
now-accepted truth that policy and administration in government
are indivisible.

An interesting phase of Appleby's experience was his work in
India where he was asked by the government to make a study of
India's administrative problems. His report obtained wide acceptance including that of Prime Minister Nehru himself. He
was subsequently invited to return to give the benefit of his ideas
to the provincial governments in India. His sympathy for the
people and his understanding of their problems assured him of a
warm welcome in any work he undertook.

In this brief book, which he has called *Citizens as Sovereigns*,
he has written from his wealth of experience. I might sum it up
by saying that he has encouraged the humble, and humbled the
arrogant. He brings out so clearly the influence that citizens can
have on their government, individually and collectively, and
explodes the misconceptions of the haughty. In his first chapter,
he demolishes many of the clichés that have wide circulation
among the thoughtless. In other chapters, he gives us an understanding of the way in which our government works best. He
shows the need for an effective two-party system, and exposes the
inadequacy of local governments wherever there is one-party
domination. He also makes clear the danger of proportional
representation.

I recall a remark of Winston Churchill when I saw him in
London a week after his defeat in the election of July 1945. The
Labor party had won control of Parliament, but by a minority
popular vote. The combined popular vote of the Conservative
and Liberal parties was in fact greater than that of the Labor
party. So I suggested that if proportional representation had
existed in Britain, he would still have been Prime Minister as
the leader of a Conservative and Liberal coalition. In his strongest Churchillian manner, he said that he would resist with all

the strength at his command any consideration of proportional representation. People must be able to place responsibility on the ruling party.

Anyone who reads this book will learn much about his government, will experience some of Appleby's own rich life, and throughout the pages get to know an American citizen who has accepted his responsibilities, and thoroughly enjoyed the opportunities that our country offers.

W. AVERELL HARRIMAN

Washington, D.C.
January, 1962

Acknowledgments

A GENEROUS grant from the Carnegie Corporation has been the chief means enabling me to get this volume written. My gratitude goes to the board of the Corporation, and particularly to John C. Honey, Executive Associate.

Syracuse University and the Maxwell School there not only administered the grant most helpfully but also provided from old friends and colleagues varied and extensive co-operation encompassing research, fact-verification, discussion of substance, and editorial criticism. Special mention should be made of former Dean Harlan Cleveland, Vice-President Clark D. Ahlberg, and Professors Burkhead, Sufrin, Birkhead, Martin, and Eggers. Mrs. Elizabeth Lowe, executive secretary of the Maxwell School, extended a previously long record of helpful personal assistance to me. Professional colleagues and friends who discussed certain points or commented on drafts included Wallace Sayre, Charles McKinley, F. C. Mosher, Emmette Redford, Earl Strong, W. W. Waymack, Louis Brownlow, Dean Acheson, Florence Kerr, Robert S. Herman, and Leonard Brodsky. All members of my family served usefully as counselors. Peter R. Baehr as a graduate assistant gathered much of the detailed information on which certain parts of the volume depend.

To all of these and to many others who have been sources of

help and stimulation during the years I express my deep appreciation. Even so individualistic a task as writing an essay illustrates the institutional way of life; he who signs the document becomes responsible for it, but what he does is inevitably a product of intricate interaction between different persons, functions, and viewpoints.

P. H. A.

Preface: What a Rolling Stone Gathered

THIS BOOK is an effort to put on paper what seem to me to be the most significant learnings derived from a life now approaching its eighth decade.

Even among characteristically mobile compatriots my life has been curious. Harold Laski in one of his books devoted a paragraph to describing it as an example of the astonishing way in which in the American government persons come to rather high position for no logical reason.

Since most readers who know of my activities will be disposed to think of me only in terms of the national government, there may be some purpose in sketching the whole background.

I attended my first political rally in a small Missouri village at the age of five, in the first campaign between McKinley and Bryan. By the time I was twelve I had begun to concentrate on local affairs; I had attended a number of mass meetings, and as a newspaper carrier had observed how reform campaigns required me on Sundays to carry the paper through the back doors of saloons instead of the front doors used in quieter times in spite of the Sunday-closing law. I eavesdropped unchallenged while the politicians planned a coup which smashed one of these reform efforts.

Beginning in my twenty-second year, and intermittently thereafter for a total of about eleven years, as publisher of weekly
papers in several small communities in Montana, Minnesota,
Iowa and Virginia I covered court proceedings, council meetings,
board of supervisors meetings and political conferences in a
privileged capacity. Other journalistic work extending over a
period of eight years included four years as an editorial writer in
the state capital of Iowa.

In figures, the record goes something like this: I have lived in
twenty different communities in seven states besides the thirteen-
year period of residence in the District of Columbia and its suburbs. Of these, eight places in four states ranged in population
from 2,500 downward; six in four states had from 5,000 to 50,000
inhabitants; and five other than Washington, D.C., located in
three states, ranged from 100,000 upward. The states were in the
Middle West, the Rocky Mountain region, on the Pacific Coast,
on the Atlantic Coast, and in the Old South. I have visited all of
the states except Alaska a good many times, and know all but a
half-dozen of them rather intimately.

I have worked on middle-western farms, on a fruit ranch in the
Wenatchee Valley of Washington, and in six retail stores; since
college I have been employed in private enterprise for about a
dozen years, have been self-employed as a publisher for about ten
years and have seen dozens of sets of account books exhibited by
business men who wished to discuss their problems with me. I
worked for the national government for thirteen years. I served as
an academic dean in a private university for eight years, and
worked for the State of New York for three years.

In the course of the last twenty-four years before retirement my
activities occasioned working relationships with representatives of
sixty nations. I became personally acquainted with more than a
dozen Chiefs of State, with scores of Cabinet members, and with
thousands of other personnel on all levels of a good many governments.

The point of this recital is simply that whatever is written here
is not the result of a single major function or location. I have been
janitor, printer, farm laborer, door-to-door salesman, sales clerk,
newspaperman, business man, public official and academician. I

have run my own business, have been a salaried business executive, university teacher and dean, and government official at both national and state levels.

When I first became a public official I was forty-one years old and, although I had much earlier developed a special interest in government, my strongest commitment was to my fellows as citizens and human beings. Because of the Depression, everyone I knew was in great trouble, and I considered the invitation to come to Washington as a chance to work in our common behalf. I went as one might enlist in time of war.

Offices of department heads were not staffed in terms equal to the wholly unprecedented demands for attention and help that almost overwhelmed us. In a few months I was given a most concentrated experience in regard to citizen manners toward and expectations of officials. Widespread and deep distress caused these attitudes to be revealed in almost raw terms.

Within the course of a few months we, in the Department of Agriculture, received hundreds of thousands of telephone calls, along with more than a million letters and telegrams. Thousands of callers descended upon us. Demands on the "front office" of that one department included, of course, persistent efforts at communication by employees of the department—working with whom was the indispensable essential if we were ever to get any new programs under way or to influence the conduct of established programs.

Most of the citizens making these legitimate demands upon our time had no notion of our situation or of how to get their concerns expressed to serve their own purposes best. Nearly all of them seemed to feel that any official in the office of a Cabinet member could do whatever they wished him to do, if only he would. This is always a much more general attitude than students of government believe. The combined effect of the enormous disorder created by the Depression, the announced policy of the new Administration to restore social order and provide relief, and individual desperation caused vast numbers of citizens to make their demands personal charges upon any official they might get to see. They seemed not to be aware that Congress had to lay down ground rules, and that discretion of any official is circumscribed

by these rules and by the responsibilities and discretion of everybody else. The people wanted help, and they appealed for it in
the most direct way they knew.

The ordinary citizen was not essentially different in this attitude from those of position with presumptions of worldly wisdom.
The latter tried to get "influential" introductions, but these were
in support of requests likewise predicated upon an assumption of
unrestricted official discretion and a general inclination to do
favors for friends or friends of friends.

One of the important purposes of the systematic way in which
individual discretion is confined is to make it most unlikely that
it will be exercised by conferring special favors as such upon
anybody.

There are other valid reasons why discretion should be limited.
What government can do for anybody is arrived at and carried
out through systematic arrangements of interacting responsibilities. Even the most informed citizen can hardly appreciate the
details of these arrangements—and does not need to. But citizens
do need to understand that the arrangements are systematic, and
that responsibility and fair-dealing alike require that governmental action be methodically taken.

Citizens who do not know what to expect, what to ask for, and
how to ask for it, tend to get evasive replies. Most officials do not
want to be unresponsive, and it is actually impossible to explain
all of the reasons why most proposals are inappropriate or un-
feasible. Even if it were possible to explain fully, the usual citizen
would not attend to the reasoning very much, and would be impressed chiefly by the fact that the official appeared to be denying
his request. The citizen seeking something from his government
wants help, not explanations. When his needs are not so particular or so pressing, however, he can and should be given a very
much improved general understanding of his government. Yet
when not themselves potential beneficiaries, too many citizens
take an unthoughtful and broadly negative attitude. They then
embrace as inflexible "principles" old dogmas hostile to any new
governmental action—and do this as blindly as in other circumstances they had sought action in their own behalf.

In the course of my experience within the government I developed a deep concern about the need for an improved understanding of governance on the part of citizens. Official efforts to explain usually relate to a few, quite particular, problems or programs, only a few presidential utterances directing attention to the general social scene. The pressing concerns of political leaders bearing operational responsibilities, in other words, are not such as to lead to thinking of the kind that gave us our Constitution.

Somewhat similarly, academic formulations usually represent work of a highly specialized sort in fields and sub-fields of the various disciplines. Particular persons, functions or programs, and particular levels or jurisdictions characteristically pin-point these efforts. In a more superficial and less systematic way, the press also reports actions and offers speculations in endless staccato columns dealing with particular problems and persons.

In their turn, when citizens shift attention from their exacting private concerns to public affairs, they tend to do so in terms of their private preoccupations, in terms of a few remembered—and usually very recent—impressions, or in clichés widely accepted as "principles."

The volume of interchanges between citizens and government, like the volume of academic studies and journalistic output, goes up as the advance of civilization broadens and complicates the concerns of men. The need for efforts to deal with government in some kind of comprehensive or representative fashion seems to me to be acute. This volume is one individual's modest effort to contribute to the cause of improved communication.

One common thread in my forty-four years of adult work was an element of executive responsibility in my own small businesses or in other employment. My orientation was to the practical task of getting things done and accepted, and making ends meet. My avocation was trying to make intellectual sense out of what I did and what I saw. Hence, one preoccupation here is to record some of the relevant reflections of an administrator.

For sixteen years I was a "political executive," even though President Roosevelt said I was "practically a civil servant." I became, I suppose, a semi-professional public administrator, with high-level policy responsibilities. During those years I was a middle-man between the civil service and professional staffs, politicians, citizens and pressure groups. The final perspective reflected in these pages, therefore, is that of such a middle-man.

No doubt there are others who have been personally acquainted with more citizens located in more places and engaged in more kinds of activities than I. Many have worked longer in public jobs. Many have worked longer in private posts. Many others have more extensive and intensive academic equipment. Some persons have worked at least as much as I have in and with national, state and local governments and in international affairs. But perhaps the mixture of my worldly experience with citizens, my academic associations, and my exposure to all levels of American government and to other nations makes it possible for me to provide a somewhat uncommon and useful slant on our government and citizen relations thereto.

Whatever value this volume may have, therefore, inheres in the fact that it is some of the no-moss a rolling stone gathers. It represents a particular formulation growing out of an unusually varied exposure to the phenomena of government and a similar familiarity with many persons variously situated and preoccupied apart from government.

More specifically, this is an attempt to present in one small book a minimum of what seems to be necessary to the proper understanding of citizenship responsibilities in our system of government. For such a purpose, even though a rather comprehensive view is avowed, emphasis here must be placed on the enveloping national government.

A Bureau of the Census study of 1952 listed 116,742 state, interstate or local "governments" in the United States with independent revenue and operating powers. Counties, towns, villages, cities and special authorities are so numerous and vary so much in legal, structural and functional respects that they can be dealt with usefully only in specialized terms, or in connection with somewhat abstract discussions of government in general.

Cities, of course, vary greatly in physical size, dimension and character of population, powers, governmental structures, and suburban involvement. Allocation of functions between state, county, town, village, city and special authority does not follow any common pattern. Differences in traffic regulations experienced by motorists are less drastic than many other statutory variations.

The discussions in this essay bear upon all these various jurisdictions when they concern leadership, parties, voting, representational patterns, delegation and some other matters. The reader in a particular location, however, will need to relate what is said to his own jurisdiction. But beyond any recognizably direct bearing, there is the profoundly important relevance derived from general local dependence upon the national authority and character.

Either national defeat from without or internal disintegration within the nation would inflict enormous damage upon the states and local communities, their institutions, and their citizens. Wholly apart from the threat of external aggression and the ruinous possibilities inherent in modern warfare, national longevity has never been something to take for granted. The new problems of planetary interdependence and the accelerated tempo of social change resulting from modern technologies make the pursuit of survival enormously more complicated and difficult than ever before.

Civilizations are concerned with art, learning, moral, humane and economic matters. But their endurance is a problem of institutional performance, and the crucial instrument is government. Politically, although not in all other cultural respects, up to now we have been living chiefly on our inheritance from the British, and on the extraordinary achievements bequeathed to us by Madison, Washington, Jefferson, Hamilton, and their dedicated colleagues. We have been enjoying the benefits of our inheritance as a matter of everlasting right, as to this manna born, and turning our attention to more personal and particular matters. The social inflation inevitably associated with civilization, however, has been making our political capital ever less adequate.

The citizen of today is the Organization Man in his family life, his goods-producing, product-marketing and recreational activities. He tends, in contrast, to be the Disorganization Man in his attitude toward primary requirements for over-all social coherence necessary to private individual and institutional satisfactions.

Change is the rule in the private organizational scene, where invention, experiment and experience compound themselves. Defense of this private scene in static terms is futile, denying its real character as well as overlooking its basic dependence upon a governmental organization which is undergoing similar change.

The organization wherein sovereignty vests is always paramount. When this organization is dedicated to pursuit of democracy, and when civilization is rapidly advancing, citizens are much less regimented by new restraints than they are burdened by new scope for judgment.

During the last century and a half the rate of social change has been progressively accelerated here, its technical factors have become much more numerous and complex, and geographical involvement has reached planetary dimensions. Only through improved political and social understanding can popular sovereignty be maintained and effective under these conditions. Here is a compelling challenge to those who take their citizenship seriously —a challenge to question many beliefs they have felt to be axiomatic by exploring freshly some basic ideas about themselves and the society they control.

PAUL H. APPLEBY

Washington, D.C.
January, 1962

I

That Government Is Best--

MANY THINGS make it difficult for the citizen of a democracy to understand his government and his personal role in it. He tends to confuse his position as a subject of government with his function as one vested with power over it. The conscientious citizen is disposed to overload his own back; he does not distinguish satisfactorily between his personal responsibility, the responsibility of the public at large, and the duties of parties and officials.

In the United States in particular there seem to be four rather peculiarly important and specific barriers to an understanding of the function of democratic citizenship. They are so related to each other as perhaps to be only different aspects of a single condition.

One of these is a widespread and long-standing attitude of hostility toward government. In part this derives from our own political emergence out of rebellion against authority. In part it is a heritage of our most extraordinary and extreme pioneer background carried with us in our rapid movement out of that individualistic condition into a situation of complex interdependence. Following the brilliant performance of the members of the Constitutional Convention, there was for more than a century almost a monopoly of political theory widely dispensed

1

by thinkers temperamentally remote from operating responsibility or insight. This theory was individualistic, anti-institutional, and largely negative.

The antigovernmental attitude is reinforced by general preoccupation of citizens with nongovernmental matters. These private activities have been most extensively developed in this country through institutions vesting great power privately, thus both complicating and enriching life. They impose their own heavy disciplines with an insistence that causes us to tend to treat public concerns raggedly or to turn to them only in time of emergency.

These attitudes and preoccupations encourage us to mistake our individual notions for valid judgment of what is generally acceptable. Every day thousands of confident judgments find expression in views or proposals which responsible officials know to be altogether infeasible and unacceptable. Nothing is so illuminating of the areas of discretion actually available as active candidacies for office at the governmental levels appropriate to the policies being considered—nothing, that is, except actual service in posts of elective responsibility. Very few citizens can have the benefit of such experiences.

These three popular attitudes and conditions inimical to understanding of the citizen's role lead to a fourth one. This is a popular reliance on fixed opinions, doctrines, or dogmas which seem to make the solutions to public problems easy. The beginning of wisdom for citizens will probably come most readily when they start questioning the clichés which now too often are used in lieu of inquiry and reflection.

In the hope of stimulating re-examination of many positions long held by numerous citizens, some of the familiar clichés are here listed and questioned. The purpose is not to try to demolish these beliefs in the course of a few paragraphs; rather, it is intended to challenge them sharply enough to invite further exploration of the political realities.

1. *That government is best which governs least.*

Does this mean that the government is best which puts up the weakest defense against attack? Or the one which gives the poorest mail service? Or the one that does least about education, highways, hospitals for the mentally ill or defective, provides the least care for veterans, and lets contagious diseases spread most widely? Does it refer to the government that does least to prolong the usefulness of its natural resources, provides the fewest parks, and neglects its public domain generally? Does it mean that the best government is the one that does the least research, collects the fewest statistics, and gives no weather forecasts?

Carrying on and supervising the activities mentioned engages the services of about 85 per cent of all the persons employed by all levels of American government. We need not go on to account for firemen, policemen, street cleaners, and many others engaged in a variety of essential services to see that the slogan is a gross absurdity. The very persons who utter it are continually seeking more public services.

2. *Bureaucrats are parasitic, mediocre and wasteful.*

What bureaucrats are being indicted? The mail carriers? The firemen? The policemen? The forest rangers? The scientists in the National Institute of Health? The school teachers? The staffs of the Secret Service, the Bureau of Customs, or the Foreign Service? These are the bureaucrats. The great majority are impressive as public servants—intelligent, honest, painstaking, helpful. One can only wonder how such people can be retained for the pay they receive. The bureaucrats we indict in sweeping general terms are those we cannot identify.

3. *Power corrupts.*

A common inference from this dictum is that every president tends more and more to want to usurp power and to become a dictator. The saying is presumed to apply only to government. If it were true, it would apply to all kinds of authorities—church and business, as well as governmental.

The citizen trying to get behind this "axiom" might demand a list of specific examples or a description of particular situations in which corruption of power has developed. If not all power corrupts, we need to know in what kind of structures and in what kind of circumstances and with what kind of power-holders it does occur. In a democracy such corruption must be usurpation from within the formal government—not usurpation by revolution and conspiracy from without.

Hitler was put into the young and weak German republic from outside it by conspiracy of a powerful few, in a multi-party situation. Mussolini was a revolutionary from outside the government who had been gaining power by military means, in a multi-party, ideologically split society. The Italian democracy was at best underdeveloped, and the crucial acquiescence to Mussolini came from the king. To be able to meet emergencies is as necessary for democracies as for any other form of government. Failure to do this can open the way to usurpation of power from outside the government.

In our country, a dean of the civil service who had watched the national government critically for more than four decades told me that "the longer presidents are in office the less often they exercise power, the more they reserve it for highly important matters." The crisis of civil war conferred more power upon Lincoln than upon any other president, but with the benefit of hindsight, we now hear no serious charges that this power corrupted him or diminished our democratic character. His one exercise of restriction on civil liberties was in suspension of habeas corpus, specifically provided for in the Constitution in case of invasion or rebellion. That this curtailment of civil rights did not endure is a proper test of the "corrupting" effect of that exercise of restrictive power.

There is a widely accepted saying to the effect that every man who has become president has "grown" in that office. This cliché challenges the one affirming that "power corrupts" in all circumstances. It appears likely that power vested under a well-established democracy does not stimulate hunger for more power, but rather disposes those who hold it toward an attitude easily mistaken for timidity. This is actually evidence of the "growth" often remarked; it comes from a heightened sense of accountability. It may well be that it is *irresponsibility* that corrupts; that what we need to be concerned about is having structures and methods that fix responsibility and make those who hold it accountable.

4. *Any government impairs freedom; freedom exists only in the absence of external restraint.*

For sheer nonsense this cliché would be hard to surpass. There is no freedom in chaos. There is no lasting satisfaction for normal persons in isolation. Any kind of social life requires restraints, just as it poses choices not otherwise available. Both tyranny and freedom are products of institutions, and the fundamental problem concerns the form, manner, and spirit of governing institutions.

5. *Centralization is bad; decentralization is good.*

This is similar to the cliché first discussed, since to many people (though not to business executives) "decentralization" is almost synonymous with "disorganization." Actually, nothing can be decentralized that has not first been centralized. Decentralization is an aspect of, or a method often useful to, centralized social entities, including government. Delegation is one means of effecting decentralization, but it requires authority. It can be used only by a central person or a central agency capable of assigning, withdrawing and modifying the delegation. And only so can delegated action be responsible action.

Civilization itself is a pursuit of centralization. For centuries the world has moved slowly and irregularly but with great determination toward larger systems of order. In ancient times there were many more governing entities near the Mediterranean Sea than there are today in the entire world. Social relationships have similarly become more extensive, more ordered. Life has become richer and more interesting. Practically nobody, when put to the test, has actually found the "good old days" preferable.

6. *The national government has greatly encroached upon the powers and activities of state and local governments, with great damage to them and "the American system."*

Anyone who utters this cliché should be required to give at least three substantial examples of the "great encroachment"— examples of functions now nationally performed, earlier performed by the states or communities, and/or now clearly claimed and desired by the states and communities. He should be further required to give a reasonable estimate of the amount of money or the number of personnel involved in these usurped functions.

Leaving out the periods and influences of crises in war and foreign affairs, which have always been clearly in the national domain, it has been true for the last six decades (for which data are available) that state and local governments have grown about as rapidly as the national government. Generally they have grown in the same periods. It is a fact, too, that there is little widespread demand for the "return" of specific functions. It is naive in the extreme to assume that legislators geographically representative, who wish more than anything else to please their constituents, would have been blandly undermining the states and their local entities. Congress, indeed, prefers to prod and help the states to act in response to needs newly felt in terms of insights and resources newly available.

7. *Private enterprise is disappearing.*

Private enterprise as we know it is so new and developing so rapidly that this is an absurd charge. Private enterprise has no fixed character the ancient glory of which is being tarnished; it is still taking form, and nowhere has it been developing, diversifying, and increasing its scope and power so much as in the United States. Informed business leaders and students of business acknowledge this. Many of them also agree that the growth of private enterprise has been consciously and carefully nurtured by western governments, and by the government of the United States most of all. Some are uneasy about this admission, however, and many qualified spokesmen for private enterprise contend that while government has not done them much wrong so far, it may tomorrow, or next year, or next administration.

An American millionaire, who came to this country as an immigrant from England when he was a young man, made this remark at about the time of his retirement from business: "There is one thing I can't understand about my American business associates: it seems to be almost a part of their business to be opposed to the government, while in England all businessmen assume before anything else that the government is in fair share their own instrument and that they must defer to and work with the government."

This man is as thoroughly conservative in his political views as all but a handful of his wealthy colleagues in business and industry. His disagreement with them is almost entirely limited to the matter of hostility versus a sense of dependence upon and membership in government. He has an advantage in having seen, recognized, and reflected a bit upon two different attitudes.

8. *We are more regimented by government every day—especially by the national government.*

The total number of restraints exercised by government increases with the number, scope, and complexity of private relationships and concerns accompanying the advance of civilization. Traffic regulation was much simpler when there were no automobiles. Increased population multiplies interpersonal relationships, so that more city ordinances and regulations are needed in New York City or in Chicago than in Emporia, Kansas. But the owner of a car has powers not possessed by his horse-driving ancestors, and must exercise discretion in ways undreamed of by his predecessors. Disciplines, discretions, and freedoms are interrelated. The most constant disciplines for almost everyone are the disciplines of family, personal associates, and job. All of these confront us with new problems of judgment that greatly burden our discretion. The scope of our discretion has widened at least as much as disciplines have increased, and surely the opportunity to exercise discretion is an aspect of freedom.

Imposition of discipline is not nearly so simple, so much confined to government, or so exclusively regimenting and so little freeing and enriching, as the cliché has it. And its concluding phrase, "especially by the national government," is simply untrue. Governmental restraints are far more often imposed by local government than by national government. While compulsion and restraint are exercised at crucial points, the great bulk of governmental activity at all levels can best be classified as public services which are sought by citizens and in general are essential to the existence of a society as highly developed as ours.

9. *Big government is inevitably worse than small government.*

If we are to take this glib generalization seriously it simplifies comparisons of very unlike institutions. In such terms, the Dominican Republic has a better government than the United States; so have Cuba, Nepal, Bhutan, Korea, Ecuador, and many other countries. Yet this is not widely believed, even outside the United States.

Governments are properly to be judged and compared in terms of the values they seek, the resources they have, their rates of development, their security from outside competitive thrusts, their processes, and a great many other elements. A big government can certainly resist aggression more readily than a small one. It can do much more. A vital question is what the people of a particular country wish their government to do.

Where competence in directing large institutions grows, what would have been regarded as a big government by the citizens a few years ago is a government of moderate size today. Size is relative to need and capacity. Too many people limit their own and their government's capacities by "thinking small." They espouse intellectually the position reached in practice by the operator of a popcorn stand whom the late George Peek, middle western industrialist, used to tell about. The man had had for years a stand near the gate of a large factory building, was well known to and liked by the employees. He suddenly dropped out of the picture. Months later, Peek encountered the man on a downtown street, and asked him what had happened. "It was this way, Mr. Peek," said the former popcorn man. "You know I had a nice business. I got along fine for years. Then I overextended myself; I took on peanuts."

Some people cannot, at a particular stage, manage peanuts. But mankind in general has shown enormous powers for expanding activities, especially by enlarging institutions and developing managerial skill.

10. *Democracy is possible only at the local level.*

This saying is close kin to the one immediately preceding it. When it does not simply reflect thoughtlessness it has emerged more out of personal insecurity than from intimate insight into life in small communities. The small community offers some significant values, but special bent toward and capacity for democracy is not one of them.

Thomas Jefferson is often invoked as authority for belief in smallness and in the special or exclusive applicability of democracy to small jurisdictions. Yet Jefferson continually expressed hope for the quality and endurance of our government because of his confidence that it would grow greatly in size and in population and thus be enabled to subordinate "local egoisms."

Like many other parts of the world, India for centuries had, more or less regardless of occupying powers, "local self-government," but not democracy. The villages of India are the greatest strongholds of the caste system. Apart from that, the local power went to the moneylender, or to a small oligarchy on which the rank and file were in overt or covert ways dependent. A New England town meeting had some engaging aspects, but held once a year or so could not transact much business; a good deal had to be done between times, and in the meetings themselves much had to be referred to committees. The basic political equality which in less closely interdependent jurisdictions can be expressed in free per capita voting and in relatively free discussion, in a small community is restrained by familiarity of the participants—the employer, and the uncle who is president of the bank, for examples.

Single-party jurisdictions are so general in small communities as to testify to something more than homogeneity. They suggest some kind of domination. And of course democracy is seriously impaired, if not obliterated, where there is a one-party condition.

In general, theoreticians are beginning to see that democracy in the small may in fact be hostile to democracy in the large. The idea of formalizing democracy is for the most part to be confined to government, which is by definition among all social institutions the broadest in scope. Democracy in other applications should be in terms of spirit, considerateness, and social responsibility rather than in strictly government-type structures and processes.

11. *"Red tape" entangles all who engage in public work, retarding, and often preventing, achievement.*

This notion about red tape is most firmly held when the government fails to do just what *we* demand of it, or just what *we* know to be the right thing to do. Conversely, the official who appears to be responsible for a decision we like is said to be "cutting red tape."

This latter phrase implies that a particular executive acts by cutting across institutional lots. If he actually did it constantly there would be no institution, no identifiable lots to cross. There would be only chaos and irresponsibility.

It is true that work will be handled more expeditiously in one unit than in another roughly comparable one, and that one executive may be, in a proper and responsible way, more decisive than another one. But a good executive is not one who "cuts red tape." He may once in a while see a way to improve his organization's procedures. But for the most part he is one who participates in and manages with virtuosity the systematic workways necessary to all responsible organizations.

In general the citizen needs to remember that he has more to gain than to lose from "red tape." It is the means by which responsibility is exercised, accountability is made possible, and many bodies of knowledge, points of view, and functions are brought to bear upon public action. It prevents whimsicality, conspiracy, and favoritism. It is an aspect of the administrative version of what jurists sanctify in the phrase "due process."

The intention in this chapter has been to discourage reliance on shibboleths. In furtherance of this purpose, a countervailing shibboleth is offered:

That government is best which governs best.

This may sound as though it were a real negation of the numbered clichés discussed in preceding pages. In a way, this one is true. Yet it, like the others, actually has no meaning. That is to say that it fails to tell us or "the government" what to do about any of the problems that require future consideration.

What courses of action will provide best government must be determined through the processes of politics, day in and day out, year in and year out. By relying on clichés, the citizen shirks responsibility, thus diminishing the national expectancy.

All of the widespread beliefs enumerated above, and others of similar sort, reflect an excessively negative attitude toward government which many good people have never examined critically. To provide some clarification of the citizen's roles, we turn in the next chapter to an examination of his role as a subject of government. Through such an examination we hope to see more clearly how much he is regimented, by what levels of government, by what segment of public personnel, and how his private resources and opportunities are nurtured by these same governmental powers.

II

Regimentation--

Citizens as Subjects

A RANGER-GUIDE of the National Park Service at a national monument in Arizona remarks to parties of sightseers: "It is the function of the Park Service to protect these unusual national features for—*and from*—the American people."

To keep individual citizens from carrying away pieces of petrified wood to the point where there would no longer be a petrified forest, is, of course, to impose a restraint. Those prevented from impulsively pursuing their short-time individual interests are made subject to a larger public interest. To protect a public interest in this way requires a subjection of citizens to a sovereign authority.

This single phenomenon thus reveals the citizen as a subject and the citizen as sovereign. It illustrates the general capacity of government to be simultaneously both confining and enriching with respect to citizens. It hints at the influence of structures and procedures especially developed under popular sovereignty in associating disciplines and services.

Democracy might be defined as the type of government least inclined to exercise controls except as a way of providing desirable services to more citizens than are regulated. It might be further defined as the type of government least given to either-or

11

courses of action. In other words, it is the kind of government least likely to decide simply to regulate or not to regulate somebody or some sort of action. Rather, it is more likely to decide against some kind of regulation and to justify the decision by granting a compensatory boon to those who sought the regulation. Or it may impose a regulation and simultaneously give some new benefit to those regulated.

Democracy *is* government. It does, and should, confine and control. But it does much else. Because of popular sovereignty, democratic government is less consistent than other kinds of government. While its capacity to exercise restraint is basic to its whole being, its orientation is to the aid of citizens, the enlargement and release of their capacities. The total impacts of its restraints and benefits cannot be precisely measured and compared; they are too unlike and too complex. Popular government, therefore, cannot be considered intelligently in terms of either restraints alone or benefits alone. Very often these are simply different aspects of the same governmental activity. In certain instances either or both aspects may be invoked as balancing factors in the social order.

It is easier, however, for citizens to think of themselves as subjects of the government than to see themselves actually functioning as members of a governing sovereignty. It is widely believed that any government has the single and pervasive function of so restraining citizens as inevitably and exclusively to impair their freedom. Citizens have been told so often that they are regimented by the government—especially the national government—that many have come to accept this as axiomatic.

Such notions not only ignore the constant disciplines exercised by society—the family, the job, the Joneses—but also are monumentally contrary to fact. Not only is it true that when popular government restrains citizens it generally does so with a compassion and consideration not similarly found in other institutional forms. It is also true that a very small part of government personnel and government expenditures for all levels of government in this country is used in regulation of citizens. Furthermore, the vast preponderance of regulation and restraint imposed on citizens is so imposed by local and state governments rather than by the national government. Before examining the citizen as sovereign, it may be desirable to consider his status as subject. In this respect, a brief description of governmental activities may be illuminating.

Categories of Governmental Activities

Although it is difficult to establish clear categories of governmental activities, the major aspects are represented in the following seven broad areas.

The simplest of the government's activities involving dealings with citizens is probably the *buying of goods and services.* Letting construction contracts, entering into leases, contracting for aircraft, missiles, typewriters, and many other things, the various levels of government engage annually in millions of transactions in which relationships are very much like those between buyer and seller in the strictly private realm. The government specifies requirements, those who seek to get the business make offers in those terms, and firms to whom awards are made presumably profit thereby as a rule. This surely is not what is meant by complaints about "regimentation."

There are other millions of transactions involving *negotiation between government and citizens* in which the resulting contracts confer governmental benefits or privileges: use of the public domain for mining or grazing; "sustained yield-use" harvesting of the national forests; farm-loan, commodity-loan, or conservation-aid payments are for the most part worked out voluntarily for the sake of interest saving or other beneficial income consequences. Rural electrification co-operative loans, and contracts involving use of water or power developed in reclamation projects provide other examples.

An *outright provision of services* constitutes a third classification of important relationships. Fire protection, street cleaning, garbage disposal, water and sewage facilities, parks, playgrounds, school systems, weather forecasts, compilation of basic statistics, biological, chemical and physical research, the postal service, streets and highways, national defense and the management of relations with other nations—all these and many more services require no contractual negotiation and are largely free from any odious regimentation content.

Compulsory school attendance is the most extensive regulating function incident to the type of activities mentioned, and while modifications in curriculum or in ages specified in the present statutes might be desirable, the provision of the service undoubtedly is much more widely applauded than its incidental compulsion is deplored. (The compulsion in this case, it should be noted, is imposed by state governments and largely enforced locally; it is not at all a product of national government.)

The *postal service* had a much more regulatory character a century or more ago than it has now. When Lincoln was postmaster he and his fellows could and did decide arbitrarily what to accept for the mails. The establishment of second-class privileges for newspapers and magazines was definitely predicated upon their educational value, and publications felt not to meet the requirements were denied entry in that class. *Captain Billy's Whizzbang* during the early years of the present century was an example of a rather widely circulated magazine which was denied second-class entry; it was shipped by express and sold chiefly in cigar stores. The *Esquire* case a few decades later put a practical end to the original regulatory policy, and today the number of man-hours spent in regulatory work in the postal service is infinitesimal. This example has a bearing on a common assumption that regulatory practice inevitably compounds itself.

The *provision of streets and highways* also entails regulation of traffic, but, as in the case of the schools, the service afforded can be considered to outweigh the incidental fact of regulation.

A fourth category of governmental activities may be seen in those which provide a *basic order for the conduct of private activity*. Realty title records maintained by the county recorder, county clerk, or similar official, the provision of money and its management in connection with the efforts to maintain an orderly economy, a body of law and a court system to facilitate private contracts and to handle differences between citizens, maintenance of a system of weights and measures, port facilities and waterways, provision for inheritance, ordering of marriage and intrafamily rights—all of these and many more stimulate and facilitate orderly activities of citizens, rather than confining them.

Regulation appears only incidentally in connection with the *fixing of minimum standards*, a fifth category of governmental activity. Sanitary requirements for soda fountains and restaurants, admission to the practice of medicine or law, quarantines, licensing of plumbers and electricians, building codes, zoning, the fixing of standards for degree-granting colleges and universities, and for utilities, insurance companies, and banks—all these are regulatory, standard-fixing functions of state and local government. There is no agreement that these things should be done away with, even among those regulated; for most citizens these functions are regarded as helpful and protective services.

Prevention, detection, and punishment of crime similarly regulates the conduct of some citizens, while being regarded by the great majority as an essential service. A sixth category of governmental business, it may be considered tangential to the third one, in that it provides a basic service analogous to fire protection; or it may be said to resemble the fourth category, the maintenance of realty title records. It supports the integrity of property, and protects citizens from violence. It maintains minimum standards of social order. Citizens generally do not have control of crude crime in mind when they complain about being regimented. Most citizens do not want to be, or to suffer from, burglars or pickpockets, or to live where murder or manslaughter is frequent. The handling of crime is overwhelmingly left to the state and local governments, as will be made clear.

The definition of crime becomes wider, of course, with the advance of civilization, the development of deeper insights, enlarged social potentialities, and heightened standards. What had been regarded at an earlier stage as merely sharp practice may later be defined in law as fraud. The newer such an enlarged definition, the more likely is it that regulation of such practices may be regarded as regimentation.

A seventh category of governmental involvement with citizens is in efforts to *redress imbalances and inequities* resulting, perhaps indirectly, from permissible patterns of action by particular groups or society at large. In order to avoid regulating or otherwise changing the established social practices, the government often establishes programs designed to provide benefits for those whose needs are newly seen. Farm relief; subsidization of railways, ocean shipping, and silver mining; programs of slum

clearance and public housing; urban redevelopment; and unemployment insurance provide examples. These policies are not
essentially regulatory, but they entail increased taxation, record
keeping, and incidental activity. Increases in taxation and the
relative novelty of some of these programs may be responsible
for part of the general feeling that regulation of life by government has rapidly increased.

Governmental Restraints

Turning once again to the question of governmental restraints
upon citizens, let us compare briefly the number of formal proceedings brought against citizens by the state-local authority and
those brought by the national government. In a typical year
United States courts of initial jurisdiction handle about 42,000
cases of all kinds—civil, immigration, income tax, fraud, theft,
narcotics, liquor. In contrast, the Federal Bureau of Investigation
reported that in 1959 violations of state or local law brought
arrests numbering 2,612,704 in 1,789 cities.

Aside from the institution of cases in court, there are many
other kinds of procedures in which directions may be given and
restraints exercised. In a vast number of cases the decisions of
local assessors are arbitrary, unfair, final, and important to the
citizens concerned. Even the application of the national Selective
Service Act, a local function, is so frequently unfair or unbal-
anced from a wide perspective that as conservative a person as the
late Senator Robert Taft had come to favor nationalizing the
whole organization. Although these illustrations identify arbi-
trariness and unfairness, the main point in introducing them
here is to emphasize the fact that, in most drastic and in most
subtle actions alike, local government has more restraining scope
than does the national government.

At the national level there are also procedures that are not
indicated by the statistics. Many proceedings of the regulatory
agencies do not reach the courts, although the criminal charges
formally brought by such agencies and civil actions in the most
resisted instances are covered in the figures given earlier. Most
of the enforcement activities of these agencies might be called
prejuridical, and of course a great deal of pressure is exerted

effectively in the course of these efforts. It is to be remembered, however, that these functions are a minor part of the business of national government and that, considering the size and complexity of our economy, these few thousand proceedings a year are trivial in number. To be borne in mind similarly is the fact that the "citizens" against whom these proceedings are directed are almost always corporations, large enough to be regarded as engaging in interstate commerce, most of them wealthy and able to utilize the best legal talent in the country.

Large corporations are on the whole useful instruments, and breaking them up into small entities would be generally harmful rather than helpful. But because they are great concentrations of power and as such are capable of inflicting great social damage, government regulates their activities when necessary to the public interest. These large corporations that are subject to governmental control in some respect or another are the principal source of the cries against "regimentation" that are directed almost exclusively toward the national government. Their lawyers, advertising agents, and public relations officers have generally persuaded the ordinary, unincorporated citizens that the national government is everybody's natural enemy. Great corporations are practically untouchable by local government, and state powers over them are exercised with difficulty within the confinement of state boundaries. For this reason these large private interests popularize "state rights" clichés. Yet Ralph Budd, a distinguished railway president, once remarked to me that if by some freakish circumstance regulation of the railroads by the national government were to be ended, the railway companies themselves would be the first and most insistent in demanding restoration of regulation.

Without the general order provided by government there would be little scope for business. What government does in the way of regulation establishes minimum standards of one sort or another to save the more responsible businesses from the excesses of competition and to make more drastic governmental intervention less attractive to citizens. Business men in general would find it difficult to agree on any reduction in present regulation. What they fear and have feared for decades is the unknown regulation that the future may produce. In any case, regulation of business is far less drastic than the sanctions available to government which involve not corporate but personal values—arrest, indictment, imprisonment, ruined reputation, loss of decent employability.

Apportionment of Public Personnel

Another way to see the relative significance of the various functions of government is to study the deployment of public personnel. The Senate Committee on Government Operations on March 23, 1959, gave detailed figures for the national government as of January 1, 1959. A Bureau of the Census report of March 16, 1959, gave similar data for the national government for October, 1958, and reported at the same time on employment in state and local governments. Using these two reports it is possible to present a clear over-all picture, even though one in which details will not always jibe exactly because of the different dates on which the reports are based.

The Census Bureau report showed 2,405,000 civilians employed by the national government, 4,423,000 by local governments, and 1,469,000 by state governments. Eliminating employees engaged in work for the national defense establishment and for the postal service—the two largest functions, and two in which state and local governments have no payrolls—the national government was shown to have 791,000 employees, the local governmental units 4,423,000, and the states 1,469,000. The census report did not include with the Defense Department personnel others engaged in work functionally related to it—foreign affairs, the Veterans Administration, debt management, and several others. Eliminating all civilian* employees of the national government engaged in war-related work except those in the Selective Service System, eliminating all in international activities, and all in the postal service, the remainder for the national government is 563,373.

Obviously not engaged in activities the citizens have in mind when they talk about being regimented are the mint, the Bureau of Printing and Engraving, Bureau of Accounts and others of similar sort in the Treasury, the Census Bureau, Coast and Geo-

---

*There were at the same time 2,637,000 uniformed military personnel.

detic Survey, Geological Survey, Bureau of Labor Statistics, Weather Bureau, Patent Office, the Smithsonian Institution, the Farm Credit Administration, almost all of the Agricultural Research Service, Office of Business Economics, National Park Service, Rural Electrification Administration, Federal Crop Insurance Corporation, Railway Retirement Board, bureaus administering the public domain, the Bureau of Indian Affairs, the Office of Education, all but two divisions of the Public Health Service, the Congress, the judiciary, the Executive Office of the president, the General Services Administration, the Bureau of Lands in the Justice Department, the Children's Bureau, the Women's Bureau, and a handful of other miscellaneous entities.

The problem of definition now becomes more complex. What is "regulation" of a sort most or many citizens might find objectionable, and what is acceptable "law enforcement"? For the F.B.I. to pursue kidnapers or robbers of banks insured by the government is certainly not the regimentation that is objected to. Inspection of meat in packing houses not engaged in interstate commerce—widely done as a service voluntarily sought by such packers—is not regimentation. Is control of the entry of noncitizens by the Immigration Service regimentation within the meaning of the common indictment? Similarly, is plant and animal quarantine control at the national borders an objectionable, regimenting activity?

Need for a definition is also felt as soon as one considers the selective service function. Meeting the basic obligations of citizenship, as in paying taxes, is not regimentation even though the amount of the taxes paid may cause much of the outcry about governmental compulsions and restraints. Compulsory military service is an ancient institution and a continuing practice in Switzerland, often thought to be something of an ideal democracy. Yet the draft is as drastic as anything that confronts a law-abiding citizen.

The more questions one asks, the more difficult the problem of definition appears. As one way of seeking light, a graduate student who served as my assistant about two years ago made an extended effort to get responsible views of the agencies whose functions might seem to be in question. If the citizens affected reacted in a resentful way, the agency personnel would be aware of this and presumably would be able to identify the offensive characteristics of their activities. The great majority of the officials questioned took the view that their agencies had no "regulating" functions at all. Almost as frequently, the feeling was that not even "law enforcement" was involved. Under the questioner's insistence, some concessions were made. And of course spokesmen for the small agencies perhaps exclusively regulatory in nature readily confessed to that character. Under my instructions to maximize his figures, the assistant produced a list of 24,815 positions in twenty different agencies of the national government he thought might properly be considered as required for "regulating" citizen actions. These were actions which in the more or less recent past would have been generally accepted as lawful.

The resulting list follows: Department of the Treasury, 5,745; Department of Justice, 490; Department of the Interior, 5,140; Department of Agriculture, 1,240; Department of Commerce, 310; Department of Labor, 490; Department of Health, Education and Welfare, 1,585; Interstate Commerce Commission, 2,240; Federal Trade Commission, 720; Federal Power Commission, 785; Security and Exchange Commission, 910; Federal Communications Commission, 1,235; National Labor Relations Board, 1,395; Civil Aeronautics Board, 690; U.S. Tariff Commission, 225; Atomic Energy Commission, 105; Subversive Activities Control Board, 30; Federal Coal Mine Safety Board, 5; Tax Court of the United States, 150; Canal Zone government, 1,325.

In my own view, the Tax Court personnel does not properly belong in this regulatory category, and not all of the Canal Zone government persons are engaged in regulatory work (although the general character of that agency is both regulatory and arbitrary). I think the Department of Justice figure is still a bit low. There is room to argue about some of the personnel in the Federal Deposit Insurance Corporation and some of the others. But this list was conscientiously and intelligently developed and if it inadvertently understates the number of regimenting personnel by half, they still would constitute just 2 per cent of all those who work as civilians for the national government.

The above figures also suggest the refutation of a common notion that the national government has been "encroaching" upon state and local government. Defense, the postal service, post roads, customs, foreign affairs, benefits for veterans, Indian relationships, care of the public domain, territorial administration, provision of currency and management of money, the census, patents, collection of taxes, the legislative and judicial functions—all these were, of course, in the field of national government in the Washington administration. Additional categories largely reflect the advance of civilization, the possibility of new services and boons—not theft of state and local functions. Commissions have labored to produce clearly identifiable lists of significant usurpations, and have come up with little more than some weasel words.

Where Citizens Are Most Controlled—the Local Level

The government of close-up affairs has not moved away from the states and localities. The trouble there is attributable not to powers lost but to opportunities missed, needs unmet. State and local governments have grown most during the recent decades when developing technology and learning, in a shrinking world, have produced new opportunities, new necessities, and intricate interdependence at all levels—international, national, state, and local. State budgets reached a total of about $27 billion—ninety times the total for 1900—in the fiscal year 1959, and the volume of state laws, county and city ordinances, and local budgets has experienced the same kind of expansion.

It is the local government that, under state authority, has most to do with crimes of the kinds common and widespread. It is local government that has most to do with the problems of propinquity, frequent interpersonal dealing in close proximity, where shoving of one kind or another is much to be expected.

Persons residing within the same community deal with each other with an enormously higher frequency than they deal with citizens of the United States generally. They deal with persons in the state of their residence, as a general rule, very much more often than with people in nearby states, and still more frequently than with persons in remote states. It is much more difficult and costly, and much less satisfactory, for troublesome matters to be handled between persons who are residents of different states. For the entire United States, national courts handled private cases arising out of "diversity of citizenship" ranging in numbers from only 19,123 to 25,709 in each of the four years ending in 1958.

Multiplicity of dealings results in calls for the establishment of rules of conduct in such things as provision and maintenance of sidewalks, snow removal, use of fireworks and guns, sanitation and health, zoning, building codes, and electrical and fire-proofing standards.

Yet even at the local level the ordinary citizen has little real sense of being regimented, and would be hard put to it to name many objectionable restraints. The inevitably close involvement of local government with crude crime is a constant invitation to police corruption, aggravated by a lack of no-strings-attached funds for political parties. This points not toward regimentation but toward inadequacy and backwardness in local government, for which there are other important reasons.

Poor representational patterns that emphasize wards, precincts, and districts at the cost of a more general public interest, and the rapid spread of urbanization, which produces problems for which there are no proper governmental jurisdictions, are two of the important causes of deficiencies in local government, augmented often by absence of real two-party systems and the lack of close voter-and-party relationships.

In smaller jurisdictions political vitality is impaired by re-straints on inquiry and debate growing out of local intimacies and dependency relationships. Employer-employee involvements, those of neighborhood and social life, and others concerned with financial commitments retard free scrutiny of local government and deflect criticism toward the national government.

New York City, as Wallace S. Sayre and Herbert Kaufman have brought out in their important study (*Personnel Administration in the Government of New York City*, New York, 1952) is more truly democratic and on the whole better governed than any of the other large cities. Its cosmopolitanism, the vitality of civic groups, and its very size would appear to make for this superior-ity. It is the most governed of local communities; yet citizen complaints there are not generally directed against "regimentation" but against inadequate service.

As this chapter has illustrated, then, governmental regulation is actually much less significant than popularly charged, and the part played by the national government in this respect is a minor one compared to that of the local and state governments.

III

Life in a Free Society

THE IMPORTANT and pressing problems of government in the United States have to do with citizens as sovereigns rather than with citizens as subjects. The consequences of popular sovereignty are not confined to government, however. Just as nongovernmental activities and interests directly and indirectly affect government, so does a particular kind of government affect nongovernmental affairs, sometimes by regulation, sometimes by example, sometimes by service. The sovereign thus needs some general understanding of his society and of the structures, mechanisms, and management of government. This chapter gives attention to the situation of citizens as members of a free society.

"Local self-government" and either "freedom" or "democracy" are not synonymous. Indeed, local self-government may be authoritarian. It is a vehicle of free people only when designed and operated consciously and systematically to serve the values of freedom, which is more than a government-and-citizen phenomenon. Freedom, to be meaningful, must be achieved and experienced socially as well as governmentally. This may be done in part as a direct consequence of governmental discipline, and in another part as an indirect result of the environing government.

Shoppers who find salespeople in one store uniformly more attentive and helpful than those in another will usually find on inquiry that the management of the first store is notably considerate of its employees. A society in which the government is committed to the protection of civil rights and to popular accountability for its actions will have relatively more stores with considerate sales staffs, more families characterized by mutual consideration, more persons and institutions whose actions are distinguished by sensitiveness and compassion.

Institutions may be differentiated according to such characteristics, as cultures and persons may be. Margaret Mead in her anthropological studies found the people of two cultures in almost identical physical conditions, with almost identical inheritances, sharply different. One society was extremely co-operative, the other extremely competitive. These differences reflected different types of leadership in prior times, and perhaps different kinds of crises, resulting in different social structures and conventions as binding as any body of laws.

In the case of a primitive society, the distinction between what is generally cultural and what is political can be made only by an observer. Such an observer would come from an advanced society where the distinction already has been formally and consciously established and government functionally so specialized as to permit intellectual abstraction of the "political" out of the cultural whole. Governance, family and community life, religion, and the economy are intertwined in the primitive culture. In advanced cultural forms government became specialized and in a sense separate, somewhat as spinning, weaving, dress-making, tailoring, lard-rendering, and a host of other things were transferred from family and clan household life into commerce and industry.

The abstraction from a "culture" of the idea of over-all control for the sake of making general social sense, its verbalization as the conception of "sovereignty," and its unchallenged functional assignment to political government comes rather early in any consciously advancing and enlarging society.

But the influence of nongovernment upon government and of government upon nongovernment is a continuing, if varied, phenomenon. It is in the interaction of the nongovernmental activities with each other and with government that a free society is either achieved or lost. The separation noted by the observer with special experience, or achieved in a constitution, is not absolute, clear-cut, or unchanging. In a free society, similarly, a householder who had transferred functions to the general economy may recapture some of them in a "do-it-yourself" effort. It is a feature of the free society that the citizens may call upon government for new services or to abandon old ones, may use one nongovernmental medium or another for some chosen end.

In the American society rather more than in any other, while freedom is commonly, and erroneously, thought of as freedom from all restraints, concern is almost exclusively directed against restraint by government. Yet restraints exercised privately are often more constant and harsher than any others, and life here today is highly dependent upon private organizations with very great power. From 125 to 150 industrial giants control half of the total manufacturing output. About 500 of the largest business units are responsible for nearly two-thirds of all economic activity apart from farming. These organizations could not exist without the sheltering arm of government, and on the other hand the impact of their powers would not be tolerable if they were not susceptible to general influence and sometimes to specific control by means of government.

The attainment and maintenance of a free society depend first of all upon its political structures, processes, and purposes or commitments. It does not follow, however, that this entails application of the forms and practices of popular government to the nongovernmental scene. The perfecting of such devices as collective bargaining, for instance, can make more sense in the private area than systems of "employee sovereignty."

The chairman of the sociology department of a university once sent me a mimeographed statement affirming at length a belief that no one but a sociologist had any "right" to exert any influence over a sociology department. If this were so, it would follow that no sociologist would have any right to influence anything except sociology departments. The idea of "democracy" being applied in this way to successively smaller functional fields becomes rapidly absurd.

Jefferson, contrary to common impressions, saw this and wrote in 1795: "I suspect that the doctrine that small states alone are fitted to be republics will be exploded by experience. . . . Perhaps it will be found that to obtain a just republic . . . it must be so extensive as that local egoisms may never reach its greater part." In the same vein, he wrote in 1817 on fuller reflection: "I have much confidence . . . that the larger the extent of country, the more firm its republican structure, if founded, not on conquest, but in principles of compact and equality."

Freedom Under Discipline

Freedom is not the fruit of disorganization and is not the absence of discipline or restraint.

One with a large vocabulary can develop mental concepts beyond the grasp of one with less verbal equipment, and can express himself more fully and effectively. But skill in language is developed through discipline. Similarly, through the disciplines of the fine arts individuality may be enriched and given expression.

The physicist-anthropologist Malinowski (in *Freedom and Civilization*, New York: Roy Publishers, 1944) had extraordinarily penetrating insights into the nature of freedom. He saw it as significant in action, with spiritual freedom coming as a by-product of freedom in action; he saw it as meaningless in terms of a solitary person, since one man's power may be another's slavery; he saw that freedom must be predicated, therefore, in terms of groups in co-operation, using material goods, whether implements or consumer goods. He concluded, then, that freedom was to be defined as "the smooth and effective as well as successful, run of an activity undertaken by a group of men who with a clear aim in view combine for the task, fit themselves out for action and achieve the desired end."

Malinowski added that in every case full freedom implies "not merely submission to duties, development of skills and making prolonged efforts in hard work and discipline, but also gaining the rewards which result from the activity." He then came to the climactic point: "The real instrument both of freedom and oppression is always the organized partial constituent of a community: the institution; . . . freedom of . . . personal purpose and its pragmatic success is always a by-product of the freedom of institutionalized activities." Freedom, then, depends upon the design of social structures, and their management.

Comparison of various societies indicates that freedom is enhanced by the use of a variety of organizational forms from which emanate diverse influences and in the use of which are to be found numerous values. It is not simply a matter of government and private enterprise, or government, private enterprise, family, neighborhood, and church. There is room in between the outer limits of an enfolding general order for many gradations in kind of constituency, function, form, procedure, and satisfactions. Mankind invents and uses many instruments.

This is illustrated in one way by a snapshot view of a small county seat in Kansas with which I became acquainted in the 1920's. Aside from an assortment of shops and stores with single or double-lot frontages, every other physical feature of this rather typical place of about three thousand population represented functions and interests outside the private-enterprise pattern. The courthouse, the fire department, city hall, and jail, the public and parochial schools, the priest's residence, the city park, the city cemetery, a co-operative grain elevator, the various churches, the Masonic Temple, the Knights of Columbus clubhouse—all these enterprises, of course, were peripheral to the conventional business economy, but all were more noticeable than any of the profit-seeking establishments. Two decades later in that little city, as in others like it, a public airport, a Veterans' Building, a hospital, a library, and a country club could have been added to the list.

Business itself is much more varied in form, method, and control than is often recognized. The mutual savings associations and insurance companies are as vigorously led as are the stock companies, and they are only one feature of an enormous shift away from the early pattern of owner-operated enterprise. The largest industrial, financial, and commercial corporations are now usually owned by numerous stockholders and controlled by self-perpetuating hierarchies of professional managers. Vast investments from pension and insurance funds further diffuse ownership. Many important businesses have taken on a "utility" character, seeking stable returns rather than large and speculative profits.

Business today not only has many forms and orientations; a large part of it seeks also to earn public goodwill by carrying social responsibility for good personnel practices, gifts to colleges and universities, and general participation in deserving causes. Some of these many developments are clearly by-products of political democracy and the consequent change in social attitudes that go far to render obsolete the social injustices depicted by Dickens and Marx.

These things are accompanied by a new respect for personal privacy, the very conception of which is peculiar to the modern age. Primitive society not only offered a much narrower range of functional identification; it also was characterized by a kind of pueblo intimacy common today among low income populations. No census figures are available showing the number of homes in the United States where there is a separate bedroom for each child, but the total surely exceeds a million, and that this is a recognized goal is indicative of much heightened respect for individuality.

A related phenomenon is the readiness of our people to petition for attention to some cause or need, or otherwise to associate in common interest. There are those who agitate about heart trouble, while others concentrate on cancer or mental health. Sportsmen, carpenters, coin or stamp collectors, people who own automobile trailers, men named "George," fruit producers, wool growers, bankers, accountants, girls six feet tall, antique car owners—almost everyone but the daughters of frontier cattle thieves have found satisfactions in associating to talk glibly about themselves, their common concerns, and drafts of resolutions.

Another feature of a society distinguished by political democracy is physical, functional, and status mobility. Mobility in terms of residence has been greater in the United States than anywhere else because of the availability of the tremendous frontier at a time when advancing technology made it readily penetrable, and this has furthered mobility in other terms. Increase in the tentative and temporary character of hierarchical status, abandonment of inherited rank as a general determinant of political status, and extensive dissociation of economic and political leadership—these things have multiplied places of repute and influence and have made for ready movement of individuals from one status to another.

Men born in log cabins have become presidents, others born in poverty have become millionaires, children of the illiterate have become college professors, and members of a single family have gone into as many different occupations and social and economic situations as they themselves number. Conversely, children of the eminent have become nonentities, and there is a saying that families go "from shirtsleeves to shirtsleeves in three generations."

This kind of social mobility has been compounded by the mobility in location already mentioned. My own paternal and maternal forebears came to this country before the Revolution, and their descendants are probably to be found in every state; in three more recent generations the immediate members of my family have lived in twenty-six of the states, from New England to Hawaii, from northern tier to the deep South. Physical, functional, economic, and political mobility thus gives many meanings to status, offers many different kinds of distinction and many paths for individual development.

With something approximating or at least aimed toward equality at the polls, this complicated and changing society offers many ways in which influence is differentiated. Students of society used to talk a good deal about societies with—or without—a "middle class," and about the crucial importance of that class. What has been described is something much more complicated and valuable than a middle class. It is a society with a "well-filled-in social hierarchy," but with positions in that hierarchy not coextensive with the society and not nearly as permanent as the conception of a class structure assumed. People exercising leadership in a particular field wax and wane in social eminence as the function they represent gathers or loses importance. They have eminence in their field, too, only on a tentative basis because of the relatively high mobility of people in most fields in our kind of society. Position "turn-over" is one term for this phenomenon.

Among other functions, this social hierarchy of differentiated responsibilities and status positions provides channels of communication within and between fields. It gives a certain important but limited coherence to the whole society and differentiates citizens politically in innumerable ways. We are not a society of upper, middle, and lower class. We are not a society of "people" and "leaders." The people have many gradations of leaders and many avenues for leadership. Leaders are numerous, varied, limited, and temporary; in our society all leaders are nonleaders in many matters, a great many have some kind of leadership, and nearly everybody some leadership potential.

The advances of knowledge, technology, and population have been accompanied by the development of new disciplines; new, innumerable, and various institutions. The changed way of life from that of pioneering, only a century or so ago, called for a quick shift from rugged and rather isolated individualism to a high interdependence. It poses problems of discretion and judgment altogether unprecedented in scope, significance, and number, thus calling for constant and complicated exercises in the use of freedom.

The general result to be sought and cherished is a society in which everybody influences everything slightly, presently or potentially, and nobody influences much of anything very extensively or finally. Differences in influence go along with differences in responsibility, of course. The individual has relatively large powers over himself and, secondly, within his family. But in any proper family each member is a restraint upon every other, and all are affected by particular bread-winning involvements, as well as by the community, the neighborhood, the larger economy, and the political society. Officials have special responsibilities for public policy and governmental action, but they must defer to each other, they are subject to multiple citizen influences, and they are popularly accountable.

The spread of influence through the complexities of an advanced civilization and the accountability that goes along with special responsibility are phenomena of social organization and social skill. "The real instrument both of freedom and oppression is always the . . . institution," said Malinowski in his book referred to earlier. A free society is, in considerable part, an *indirect* consequence of a government dedicated to freedom and made popularly accountable. But this can be true only so long as there is sufficient skill on the part of citizens in using institutional instruments, and enough determination to uphold the government through which these other instruments are made feasible.

Life in an Organizational Complex

The multiorganizational society has many characteristics, uses, and potentialities. It provides its members with a choice of activities, a choice of means of expression, influence, and status achievement in numerous hierarchies. It makes available many goods and services in great variety. It offers facilities conducive to maximization of personal development and differentiation of individuality.

Personal development of a very significant sort may be achieved by a choice of activity which takes one into a function or a position that provides something of a niche rather than high rank. For a teacher, a scientist, or an artist fulfillment may be found wholly apart from eminence in any formal hierarchy, even though increasingly these activities also are carried on in, are dependent on, or are associated with, hierarchical structures. Satisfying a craftsman's sense in one instance and finding identification and mission with associates or students in other instances are illustrations of the values of "lateral" placement within a hierarchy.

"Identification with associates" may come from a sense of congeniality with persons of similar backgrounds. It may come through an almost opposite situation—as in the case of the one professionally trained engineer living in a small county seat town feeling at home because there he has clearly separate identity based on his profession.

In contrast to these numerous, valuable, and various niche-seekers are the relatively few who are willing to assume heavy organizational responsibility and who pursue the values that go with "vertical" placement within a hierarchy. In an intermediate category are those whose status in large organizations is rather stable at places of modest eminence, or whose memberships are preferably in small organizations where responsibilities are not too onerous. In a vast variety of organizational forms citizens seek and find satisfactions according to their interests and needs.

The patterns of organizational involvements are the products of multiple memberships in one respect, and of different manners and degrees of involvement in another. This is to say that a person does not have a single kind of membership, does not adhere to them all equally, and does not treat any one organization in a wholly unvarying manner. Most of us, in considerable part unconsciously, play a long organizational keyboard with considerable virtuosity in producing a kind of social harmony for ourselves.

The artistry of this performance relates usually most directly to general social interests rather than to government. This whole field may be regarded as the general background of the political. Artistry herein involves: maintaining or having access to nominal or loose memberships in areas or at times when concern in the interests and activities of the particular organizations is slight; changing the amount of time, energy, and responsibility utilized through any medium as occasion seems to require; relying on leadership in some matters, to some degree, and on some occasions; striving for and exerting leadership where one's concern is great; utilizing experts (doctors, lawyers, bankers, teachers, mechanics, electricians, etc.) on a good many occasions, and deferring to the judgments of these experts sometimes and to some extent.

The organizations now being referred to are families, churches, schools, colleges, industries, banks, stores, service agencies, middlemen, bar, medical, dental and other professional organizations, chambers of commerce, manufacturers' associations, lodges, country clubs, trade or industrial unions, farm organizations of general and special sort, luncheon clubs, alumni associations, and many more.

Varying degrees of involvement in memberships and choice of memberships, choice of profession or job field, choice of wife or husband, choice of clothes, newspapers, house furnishings, recreational activities, magazines, books, radio and television programs, stores to patronize, particular makes of products—all of these and very many more choices constitute extensive and numerous areas for the exercise of discretion.

The wage or salary earner who knows of another job he can

have, if he elects it, has not only heightened security but a sense
of emancipation. If two or three or more jobs are available he is
most extraordinarily free in one primary respect.

These memberships and choices are vehicles of self-expression
and self-development, of supply and security. But enlargement
of discretion may heavily tax judgment. Each membership also
entails a discipline of its own, the weight of which varies with
the extent of one's commitment to the particular association—the
degree of responsibility one assumes in and for it. The sense of
being burdened by a discipline varies also with one's sense of
dependence upon the various organizations. The organization
from which one's income is derived, one's assigned function
therein, and the family, normally impose the heaviest and most
constant disciplines.

A very lowly worker in some large organization may be so
completely dependent upon it for a living income that he gives
to it every bit of energy and loyalty—or worry—of which he is
capable. Concern for his family and for his job may be only
minutely and partially separable in his mind and emotions. Yet
there are other and divergent or comprehensive responsibilities
which he recognizes on occasion, and to which, in crisis at least,
he may give preference.

Any particular one of the memberships a citizen maintains
fails as an adequate means of expressing clearly and consistently
the particular member's sentiments. He may belong to a county
branch of the Farm Bureau. He may feel that the officers are
well chosen and deserve to be regarded as competent. Yet when
he hears certain public pronouncements they make, he feels himself to be somewhat misrepresented. The Farm Bureau organization of the state even more often will not express *his* position or
reflect *his* judgment of priorities. And the national Farm Bureau
Federation leaders may, in his view, go still further astray. Yet
on balance he still may feel quite strongly that the Farm Bureau
represents him usefully, if not precisely or comprehensively.

Similarly, union members in recent years have been seeing
perhaps more clearly than earlier some of the difficulties in the
way of getting satisfactory leadership, and in any case they have
long known that what the leaders gave them was a sort of general

voice that served a purpose but failed to represent the full range of member interests and attitudes.

These things are inevitably so. Members individually range in sentiment and concern much more widely and variously than an organization can or should do. It has a special function, and in performing it the organization will seek to find courses of action generally acceptable, since the members do not in fact have a single position. Leadership of any organization acts within a zone of membership consent rather than one of consensus. The zone almost always includes large areas of membership indifference or uncertainty wherein leadership is given the benefit of the doubt. The central fact is that the organization as such will do something that tends to reflect a common denominator position of its members, varying on one side according to the depth of feeling and confidence of judgment of the responsible leaders, on another side according to the influence exerted on the leaders by members, modified altogether to take account of what is found to be feasible in the social context.

On the Frontiers of History

This organizational complex with its great pluralism, high interdependence, and numerous problems, with many and wide-ranging choices to consider, is a new stage of civilization. We are occupying new social frontiers as rapidly as we have populated the continent.

Only one lifetime ago it was usual for marriages to be confined within single religious denominations and within a common pattern of daily life—young farmers marrying farmers' daughters living nearby, or at least members of the same community, possessing similar outlooks and following established behavioral patterns. So simple a statement must be considered in connection with the profound contrasts resulting from a later series of related phenomena: rapid immigration from more and more societies; equally rapid expansion over a deep and virgin physical frontier; rapid application of new technologies and new wealth to vast natural resources; rapid spread of various degrees of free-thinking and loosening ties of old social disciplines; easy escape from old associations and ready availability of a kind of irresponsible anonymity, first in frontier solitudes and later in urban crowds; an economy so rapidly expanding as to provide rich resources for acting in unfamiliar and often unpatterned ways; marriages undertaken across wide background gaps; novel functions of great diversity confusing and hampering communication; a bombardment of printed words about all manner of new activities; elevation of entertainment and salesmanship as most enviable of all ways to make a living; concern about popular sovereignty tending to overwhelm leadership and elevate demagogues; lengthened reach of military arms and tensions.

Surely these things are related to the advance of civilization. Taken a bit more slowly, with more conscious emphasis on responsibility, all or nearly all of these developments would certainly be truly enriching. Taken all together at the speed with which they have confronted us, they have posed for the people of this country problems of social maturation in dimension and content much greater than have confronted any other people at any time. The combination and rapidity of developments has greatly strained our capacity for poise.

However numerous and serious may be the problems that chiefly preoccupy us personally in our familial and occupational involvements, we realize insufficiently, except belatedly in crisis, our basic dependency on the instruments and processes by which alone can be maintained a general social order.

The point is that a free society tends to sprawl, rather than to be too unified. It is also true that all government is subject to competition, internal and external; that it is subject to debility and decay; and throughout the world and during all of what is known of history sovereign governments have been highly impermanent, with governmental expectancies reduced as the tempos of change in their societies have been increased. Ironically, some of the very achievements which have lengthened the span of human life now put new difficulties in the way of longevity of states.

In various ways, governmental adjustment must be an inevitable consequence of private development. Private initiative is privately manageable only because there is unconscious confidence that government will facilitate its incorporation into the social totality and make the consequences tolerable.

The United States is a young government and an experimental one. Yet even now it is the next-to-oldest continuous government in the world. Its longevity cannot be taken for granted. It is dependent upon keen popular realization of the government's primary importance and the development by citizens of competence in their sovereign responsibilities.

Professor Charles E. Merriam (reprinted in *A Study of Power*, Glencoe, Ill.: Free Press, 1950), wrote a quarter of a century ago in terms of the "poverty, morbidity and mortality of power." He cited race, religion, and class as likely sources of disaffection of the "most serious description." Again, he called attention to the Marxian attack on the state as the tool of capitalism, while capitalism attacked it as a menace to private enterprise. (So long as the statement is understood to apply only to democracies, Russian leaders certainly would unanimously endorse the policy of the *Wall Street Journal* as stated by its editor, Vermont Royster, and quoted later by John Brooks in *Harper's Magazine*, March, 1959: "Basically, we are for minimum government. We believe that the primary reason for government is to provide police power—to keep me from knocking you over the head.") Merriam went on to point out that the doctrine of laissez faire was directed toward the limitation of government powers and against the limitation of business powers, constituting an ideology in direct competition with sovereignty.

Walter Lippmann (in *The Public Philosophy*, Boston: Atlantic-Little, Brown & Co., 1955) much more recently expressed very particularly the deepest concern about the capacity of western democracy to survive. His fear was directed at the subordination of leadership to the mediocre concerns and prejudices of the masses. Not unnaturally for one of his intellectual powers, he exaggerates the importance of logic in decision-making. He also confuses individual and public judgment, finds institutional processes impenetrable, and generally underestimates politics. But his basic concern for democratic survival is certainly warranted when he says: "It will not do to think poorly of the politicians and talk with bated breath about the voters. No more than the kings before them should the people be hedged with divinity."

Still more recently, Robert Heilbroner (*The Future As History*, New York: Harper & Brothers, 1960) has brilliantly challenged our complacency from a quite different point of view in which he puts social forces and social intelligence in common focus: "Having reached an objective, what we encounter is not the 'progress' we anticipated but a new set of problems stemming from the very advance itself . . . . The painful evolution beyond present-day capitalism is indispensable if those nations which have gained the benefits of material wealth are now to cope rationally with its administration." In other words, we can defend what we have achieved only if we imaginatively face and manage the problems consequentially seen. We cannot live by the slogans of yesteryear.

Leaders may be expected so to live up to their responsibility in the relatively extreme democratic conditions obtaining in the United States today only if the people understand their own situation and learn to give more of their adherence to Lincolns living and not merely to Lincolns dead. Without surrendering critical faculties and their exercise, with less extravagance and more restraint, with ordinances of self-denial appropriate to their high responsibility, citizens urgently need more political maturity.

If "the real instrument both of freedom and oppression is always the organized . . . institution," and if the enhancement of even private and personal freedom is both directly and indirectly dependent upon the central institution—government, those citizens who would be sovereigns and free need a basic understanding of the design and management of political structures. Too many inherit their political attitudes exclusively from Samuel Adams and Patrick Henry. Useful these two were in securing colonial independence, but they opposed the Constitution. The idea of popular sovereignty has no real meaning for their political heirs. Citizens who would live up to their sovereign responsibilities must utilize and augment their inheritance from Madison, Washington, Hamilton, Jefferson, Franklin, and their colleagues who designed and led our nation at its beginning, and from Lincoln, who understood their achievement and provided the leadership essential to its preservation.

What are the elements of our political inheritance most crucial to its aspiration? Which of these elements are, instead, merely products of their time and place, or mere verbal attributions with a certain limited usefulness but far from absolute and inflexible relevance? The next chapter reflects on these questions.

IV

Our Forefathers' House

ALL SIGNIFICANT inventions, social or physical, are difficult and speculative, even though nothing is wholly new, but grows out of past forms and experience. To design and manage a substantially new industrial company is much more difficult than to operate one long established. Basic social institutions of marked novelty are very much harder to produce. It is our great good fortune in this country to be the heirs of the most notable group of political inventors the world has known at any one time in any one place.

The design and construction of our government were limited to the building materials here available at that time, notably the thirteen colonies newly independent of their mother country, with their people, their resources, workways, and outlooks. Deprived by distance and other factors of rights to which Englishmen had come to be entitled, stimulated to think freshly on this account, stimulated also by the influences of the Enlightenment and by the novelty of their own situation in a new world, colonial leaders put most extraordinary concentration of thought on the basic problems of governance. There was the failure of the Confederation, too, as a spur to thought and action. And there was the vital force of the trend of centuries in which the rights then belonging to Englishmen had been uniquely acquired, although even then by no means was England thereby made a full-blown democracy.

The design of any government derives from many things, and this is especially true of a popular government. History and popular attitudes would result in different governmental forms and practices even with identically written constitutions. One of the greatest democracies, Britain, has no document that can be called its constitution. Parties, statutes, the particular problems faced, many institutions, and many attitudes affect the political structure importantly. It was a part of the genius of our constitutional fathers that they produced a short and flexible document, one which, while not "settling" basic political questions, provided appropriate means for continually reckoning with those questions in the course of pursuing the general good.

It is well to be reminded in this connection that the Constitution was a group product, accepted as meaning different things by the very men who voted to establish it. It thus made possible the government in being today which means many things—not at all consistent—to its own citizens. Our forefathers left a wide door open to the future.

The "Federal" Conception

One of the commonest attributions to our government is a "federal" character. The Constitution nowhere uses the phrase or anything closely resembling it; it is something inferred by interpreters for particular reasons and applications and in this way it has a certain limited usefulness.

Actually, the principal first source of the "federalist" term was the Federalist Papers. Hamilton was the primary author of those papers, and the outstanding leader of the Federalist party at the time of our national beginnings. Hamilton wished to do away with the states. Failing that, he favored the appointment by the national government of a state governor who would have an absolute veto over actions of the state legislature. While his party took no such particular position, it is commonly described as the party favoring "nationalization of the new central government to the full extent warranted by a broad construction of the powers granted to it by the constitution, and a correspondingly strict construction of the powers reserved to the states and the citizens." The Federalist movement was certainly epitomized in the motto, *e pluribus unum*—emphasizing the emergence from many of a single entity.

Hindsight verbalizers formulated the theory of federalism as fixing sovereignty in the national and state governments together, not in either one or the other alone. At the time of the Constitutional Convention small states had concerns because they were small, and large states had other ideas because they were large. The constitutional language was a reconciliation, a compromise, not the adoption of a theory. Agreement was manifested in the general result of a nation being established, quickly implemented in law by Congress in 1889 when it vested over-all power to interpret the Constitution in the national courts.

Actually, the idea of equal representation of the states in the Senate, the chief structural feature thought to demonstrate a federal character, was presented originally by Connecticut as a logical sequel to the intrastate structure in New England, where the population was represented in one house while the towns were equally represented in the other. The New England states were not then and are not now regarded as of "federal" character because of this structural feature. Their "upperhouse" plan probably derived from the English House of Lords, which has no federal purport.

Aside from equal senatorial representation, the only thing in the Constitution suggestive of federal theory is in the Tenth Amendment: "The powers not delegated to the United States by the constitution, nor prohibited to the States, are reserved to the States, respectively, or to the people." The significant thing in this is the elimination of "expressly" before the word "delegated." That word had been in the Articles of Confederation, and by eliminating it the way was consciously opened to the nation to use "implied" powers.

Without the modifying phrase "by the constitution" in the language of the amendment just quoted, the word "delegated" might have been the strongest term in the Constitution supporting any federal theory as modernly formulated. But the reservation of unspecified powers to "the people" may have an opposite import. Were they the source of the powers "delegated"? In any case, how are the people to exercise these reserved powers? (The Preamble declares, "We the people . . . do ordain and establish this constitution," and ratification was by popular conventions, not by state legislatures.) If the people could exercise reserved powers only through the states, the concluding phrase would appear to be meaningless. Can the people exercise their powers by simply agitating for national action, or by electing to national office a party pledged to action in some new policy area?

The consideration of other so-called federal governments leads to no more certain conclusion. Such a common pattern as they have is one of judicial pre-eminence of the central courts and a general record of increasing operational powers in the national government. In Canada unspecified powers are assigned to the national government, and such federal character as is constantly visible is perhaps more related to the existence of a culturally French population almost two-thirds the size of the British-derived population than it is to provincial structures and powers as such. India, one of the new Commonwealth nations, has almost every superficial appearance of a federal form, particularly in those periods when one of its states is under Communist control. Yet in India the supreme judicial power is national, and the national government has clear supremacy in its right to take over any particular state; in any event, the state boundaries have been changed several times. In Latin-American nations having ostensibly federal forms, the reality is generally a thoroughly dominant national power.

Altogether, it seems warranted to say that all over the world so-called federal governments nearly always constitute strong national entities in which states are clearly subordinate. In them, use of some such shibboleth as State Rights can sometimes serve as a moderately useful focus for debate, but no more. Through such debate, deliberation can be required. But there is no final wisdom—nor even any clear and extensive meaning—in the shibboleth itself.

The physical growth of our country since thirteen states and their citizens first associated themselves to establish it has more bearing on the disappearing validity of the old slogan here than many may have recognized. Millions of immigrants came to the United States, not to the states as such. Mobility within an expanding area is another factor. The relevance of physical expansion was simply but vividly portrayed in the account of a debate at Kenyon College in Ohio on the South Carolina nullification ordinance of 1832, as given in Fletcher Pratt's biography *(Stanton,* New York: W. W. Norton & Co., 1953) :

It was already the leading Episcopal college beyond the Alleghanies, and as much of the planter aristocracy belonged to that communion, its sons came there naturally. But it is easy to see how the language of nullification that they spoke sounded like Chinese to the young men from the Northwest Territory who formed the remainder of the student body. The state sovereign? They hardly thought of themselves as citizens of a state at all. Indeed, many of them were not, being from areas still under territorial government. In all the Northwest Territory very few persons had been born in the states where they lived, and those few were mostly very young. The states themselves were new and experimental entities, convenient for handling local affairs, but little more. The national government, which sold people their lands, protected them from Indians, and built post roads, was the solid and permanent reality, from which favors and powers flowed down to the states rather than in the other direction.

As the nation expanded further in still other directions, the attitude Pratt described spread with it. Everyone in the Great West had come from other places, had relatives and some sense of acquaintance and basic membership spreading back toward the Atlantic seaboard. The nation was to them all a great entity; their last previous residence had been temporary, their present one might be if greater opportunity appeared over the horizon. For decades personal items in smalltown papers of western states have told of more visits to places several states to the eastward than trips to Richmond have been reported in papers of the same sort in western Virginia. The sense of national membership has largely supplanted state pride for those who have moved or traveled about the country. Enthusiasm for a new place of residence is not at all the same thing.

New states become old states, of course, and those who live in them are most mindful of what is immediately around them. Yet every year for the last ten years about five million people have moved from one state to another. These people and many of their kinfolk simply cannot fail to give their prime loyalty to the nation that shelters them all over so wide a spread.

Our government was a federal achievement at its very beginning, in that it was jointly established by thirteen political entities and their citizens. Not in conformity with any divinely inspired theory, but of necessity—as when private corporations merge—certain features of the Constitution were compromises taking account of these different entities and the sentiments clustering about them. These same factors were background elements of some weight, perhaps, in the sentiments of citizens of three splinter states—Vermont, Maine, and West Virginia—as they came into separate membership. But for persons in the other thirty-four states added over the course of years identification with the nation has been of highest importance—except as the Calhouns, for reasons of selfish and sectional interest, and some others, because of verbal preoccupations, have confused them.

With the passage of time, indeed, even in the original states there has come to be little real uncertainty about the primacy of the nation. The Civil War was decisive. Invocation of State Rights now is clearly a device by which some particular national action is opposed; emotional overtones are overwhelmingly related to the proposed action rather than to violation of a "federal" principle.

Checks and Balances

The second most common attribution to our government is a structural "separation of powers" into "three equal and co-ordinate parts." The Constitution nowhere uses such terms. If the powers were in fact fully separate we should have no organic structure, no living and operating government. The Constitution actually provides for interacting powers and somewhat unclearly differentiated responsibilities. The ablest constitution-makers and the ablest administrators avoid precise definitions of responsibility, just as the ablest jurists have tended increasingly to avoid sweeping determinations and to favor very particular decisions.

An uncertain separation of powers does characterize our government, particularly as comparison is made with parliamentary-type governments. Happily, the separation of powers is not clear, not too definite, and far from complete. Happily, too, it is not necessary to know—and no one does—whether the three branches are really equal. It is clearly valid to describe our government as one in which responsibilities are roughly differentiated and power is diffused through numerous checks and balances.

The Constitution provides that "all legislative powers herein granted are vested in a Congress of the United States," yet it establishes also the right of veto by the president, the overriding of which requires a two-thirds vote in both houses of Congress. The veto power extends to all orders, resolutions, etc., which require concurrence of both houses—everything except internal management of the business of each house, senatorial confirmation of treaties and appointments, the House's power to impeach, and the Senate's judicial power in impeachments. The Constitution also requires the president to give to the Congress from time to time information on the state of the Union, and to recommend for their consideration such measures as he shall judge necessary and expedient. He also is given power to call either or both houses into special session, and in case of disagreement between the houses concerning time of adjournment, power to adjourn them to such a time as he may think proper. Altogether, the president, in addition to having special executive responsibilities, may properly be regarded as a principal legislator. His powers in the appointment of judges also make him influential indirectly, at least, in the third branch.

In the same way, the power of impeachment, the pervasive power of purse control, the power to override vetoes, the power to make rules for the government, and the general power to legislate, and to conduct public debate and inquiry—these things give to Congress extensive executive control which approaches total control as congressional agreement becomes more complete and firmer.

Very similarly, the power of Congress to fix the number of judges and to establish inferior courts gives it a general control over the volume of business the judiciary can handle—which is an important indirect control of its very function. Its power to legislate can change the court's terms of reference and compel changes in interpretations of law. The power to impeach judges lies with Congress, also. The court, in its turn, has demonstrated power to limit the powers of both Congress and the president.

Thus the nation began with legislative powers divided between two houses but shared with the chief executive and with the judiciary; executive powers subject to judicial check, to congressional appropriations and to other legislative proceedings and enactments; judicial powers in persons approved by both other branches and confined by resources subject to legislative and executive action—all these powers bound to be influenced by subordinate personnel and popular reaction—and national power inevitably and properly subject to some deference to state concerns and state governmental actions.

In one short document the delegates to the Constitutional Convention provided for a popularly oriented entity which now has a demonstrated capacity to live, act, and grow, by making survival of any part depend upon the survival of all, and by requiring thoroughgoing interaction. The fact that all branches may claim separateness and equality but in fact are mutually dependent leads each jealously to guard but variously to exercise its own responsibility and to defer to companion responsibilities. The result is an open government, its parts mutually critical but generally coming to agreement, even though with a degree of deliberation which in the future we may not be so well able to afford. Yet it is essentially the familiar kind of organ visible in each executive department and within each branch. Any good organization has division of labor, intricate interaction, and mutual deference between its parts.

The "federal system" term was popularized by persons at various times resisting some kind of national action as a way of recruiting support for this opposing position. But it was early adopted by the jurists, and the courts somewhat more exclusively sponsored the rationalization of "three separate and equal branches." Yet the courts have not held a single and continuous position on these matters. The court doctrines have waxed and waned, and waxed and waned, and in any case were far from determining. Strong presidents have led the Congress fairly definitely on some occasions, and Congress has come to dominance on other occasions; State Rights have been upheld and denied. The presence or absence of crisis and personal attributes have been significant factors, as well as constitutional differentiations in assignments. The fact that the president is one person, whereas the legislature consists of two houses and more than five hundred persons, has an important significance. The further fact that the president is nationally elected, while members of Congress are chosen by localized constituencies, also qualifies legalistic simplifications.

Wholly apart from judicial theory, however, a popularly dedicated institution of the scope planned and needed for our national government will be characterized by great diffusion of power, great mutual deference between its elements. In modern conditions some of these features may be so compounded that the government may become too much hampered by them, may be unable to act quickly enough and decisively enough and grandly enough because of its own internal checks and balances.

Chester Barnard, writing in this connection (*Function of the Executive*, Cambridge, Mass.: Harvard University Press, 1945), accepted as real the "system of States Rights or dual sovereignty," and the "separation of legislative, judicial and executive departments." He said these things "preclude a common center of authoritative communication in American government as a formal organization." He said further that from the viewpoint of its executive functions our government is "intended to be defective." He concluded that "it is intended or expected that the requirements will be met by informal organization." By this he meant, one must presume, that we can survive only if there is much less than doctrinaire and rigid conformity with any formal theory of dual sovereignty or with any theory of "equal and separate parts" of our government. He meant that we require give and take, flexibility and bigness of mind and spirit in our leadership. He certainly meant that we need to use the political party instru-

ment, and to allow scope for executive discretion in the selection
and assignment of key executive personnel. Common party membership and association of congenial persons all having a great
sense of responsibility can unify what formal insistence on differentiated responsibilities would sunder.

The Democratic Dynamic

The significance of the establishment of the United States as
one of the great and novel governmental achievements in world
history has nowhere been denied. There has been considerable
tendency in bygone years to haggle over whether what was intended, and what was set up, was a "republican" or a "democratic" government. The difference most frequently seen in the
two terms is the difference between government by representatives—thought to be rather free from any direct popular control—
and government more thoroughly responsive to and controllable
by the public. With the passage of time the distinction has been
less insisted upon, perhaps principally because in the course of
evolution democratic character became more pronounced.

The remarkable fact is that very little in the original constitution explicitly bore upon the question of either "democratic" or
"republican" character. There was an undeniable and unprecedented citizen orientation. The Preamble—in which the purposes
were identified as "to form a more perfect union, establish justice,
insure domestic tranquility, provide for the common defense,
promote the general welfare and secure the blessings of liberty to
ourselves and our posterity"—along with experience, prior history, and practices already established in the states, set the tone
which was vaguely governing. But the document itself was
generally concerned with the bread-and-butter provisions of
governance, and with the establishment of rights of citizens as
subjects in the English pattern, rather than with precise arrangements for popular sovereignty. The Bill of Rights, comprising
the first ten amendments, spelled out with particularity basic
popular rights, principally for "subjects."

Only three paragraphs in the entire document, including the
first ten amendments, bore directly upon the values of popular
sovereignty. One of these outlawed titles of nobility as a step in

an equalitarian direction. Without definition of the term, one paragraph guaranteed "to every State in this Union a Republican form of government" and coupled this with a promise to protect each of them against invasion. Another paragraph provided that "the times, places and manner of holding elections for Senators and Representatives shall be prescribed in each State by the Legislature thereof, but the Congress may at any time by law make or alter such regulations, except as to places of choosing Senators." This paragraph offers certain possibilities, but does not clearly set forth principles of representation.

The guarantee of "a Republican form of government" to every state was a vague thing. And certainly a "federal system" and division of government into "three equal and separate parts" are not the essentials of popular government. The British government surely is now an eminent example of the democratic reality and it is neither federal nor divided into separate branches. Most democracies, indeed, are of the highly unified, parliamentary variety.

Tone and spirit of the basic covenant, popular attitudes, and prevailing practice were clearly more governing in terms of achieving popular character than the specific verbiage of the justly hallowed document. Suffrage patterns already in effect varied, but as compared with older forms were extensive. They tended toward the inclusion of all free men twenty-one years of age, even though there were some restrictions requiring the ownership of property, or literacy, or both. There was a strong aspiration toward truly popular government, the way to it was opened by the constitution-makers, early leadership contributed to it new practices and attitudes in actual operations, and an evolutionary process was begun.

Emergence of a party system here was a notable reality before it had achieved continuing form or significance in Britain. The establishment of the national presidential nominating conventions was an important embellishment at the end of the first quarter of the nineteenth century. The logic of the country's dedication brought enlargement of franchise through amendments to state constitutions, and these, together with national growth under the relatively equalitarian conditions of frontier life, combined to make suffrage more and more extensive. The Civil War and the ending of slavery made possible the enactment of amendments to the national Constitution which spelled out and generalized the basic attitude: "All persons born or naturalized in the United States, and subject to the jurisdiction thereof, are citizens of the United States and the State wherein they reside. No State shall . . . abridge the privileges or immunities of citizens of the United States." Then finally in Section 2 of the fourteenth amendment and in the fifteenth were these outstanding determinations, notable in themselves and notable also as recognizing national inclinations to democracy which "local egoisms" would resist:

Representatives shall be apportioned among the several states according to their respective numbers, counting the whole number of persons in each State excluding Indians not taxed. But when the right to vote at any election for the choice of Electors for President and Vice President of the United States, Representatives in Congress, the executive and judicial officers of a State, or the members of the Legislature thereof, is denied to any of the male inhabitants of such State, being twenty-one years of age, and citizens of the United States, or in any way abridged, except for participation in rebellion, or other crime, the basis for representation therein shall be reduced in the proportion which the number of such male citizens shall bear to the whole number of male citizens twenty-one years of age in such State.

The Congress shall have power to enforce by appropriate legislation the provisions of this article.

The right of the citizens of the United States to vote shall not be denied or abridged by the United States or by any State on account of race, color, or previous condition of servitude.

The Congress shall have power to enforce this article by appropriate legislation.

The logic of this evolution in democracy was continued by an amendment effective May 31, 1913, providing for the popular election of United States senators instead of the original "republican" method of choice by the state legislatures. Then in 1920 the logic was extended by an amendment providing for woman suffrage and giving Congress the power to enforce this by legislation.

The power given Congress to overrule state legislation concerning the method of choosing national officials, and the similar and more extensive powers conferred by the fourteenth, fifteenth, and nineteenth amendments have never been fully utilized. Nor has supervision of elections been extended suitably over party primary elections. But by these notable means the basic endowment of democratic character has been firmly established beyond dispute. Extension of the secret ballot, protection of collective bargaining and other developments heightening the sense of economic security and thereby making political discussion less risky have been a part of the same evolutionary progress.

Our founding fathers were not sure how far they could rely upon the general public. Jefferson's view was that citizens could be trusted to select leaders to be vested with operating authority, and this was about as far as any of the constitution-makers would have gone. But they provided flexibility, and kept the door open to the future. Today, we have in this country more potential capacity to impose citizen will directly upon the government than has ever been the case in any other extensive nation.

But while distrust of citizen competence as a basis for outright opposition to democracy is now rarely expressed, perversions of popular government constitute one of perhaps five principal difficulties in the way of actual democracy in modern practice here.

The perversions are distortions of the representational patterns —by gerrymandering, by failure of legislatures to reapportion or to advance necessary constitutional amendments to keep apportionment up to date, by citizen failure to develop and uphold two-party systems (which in effect disfranchises a good many people), by the practice of letting seniority determine legislative committee chairmanships, and by electoral practices (as developed particularly in Georgia) which make a majority of electoral districts rather than a majority of popular votes determining.

A second of these handicaps to democracy is the excessively

confining application of the "federal" idea, State Rights, and other such theoretical formulations as a way of opposing the popular will on particular issues.

A third difficulty is provided by an inclination to overload the citizen with unmanageable responsibilities through unduly long ballots, popular referenda, initiative processes, and, occasionally, the popular power to recall judges.

A fourth difficulty is of an almost directly opposite sort—a widespread slandering of "politics" which has led to taking too many functions "out of politics," resulting in irresponsibility of public agents and governmental imbalance. This movement has even gone to the extreme of advocating or establishing (in appearance) "bipartisan" or "nonpartisan" municipal government.

A fifth difficulty has been posed by the very advance of civilization, which inevitably results in increasing the technical character and general complexity of society and government.

To recognize these difficulties, to be vigilant to reduce the first four and to improve understanding of the fifth in order to make popular sovereignty enduringly manageable—these should be major aims of citizens who prize democracy. The first duty of citizens is to make it possible for a majority to dictate to their government. The second duty is to realize the way in which complexity increases disproportionately for every cultural mile civilization advances, and, in this realization, to enact sensible ordinances of self-denial in deferring somewhat tentatively and always temporarily to the agents in whom they vest the special responsibilities of official leadership.

V

Lean-To's and Other Additions to Government

THE GOVERNMENT built by our forefathers was designed for easy enlargement and adaptation. Growth and development of the society were naturally expected to call for additions to and changes in the government. Some of these changes have been as functional and comfortable as the gabled rooms and facilities attached successively to older portions of New England houses as families grew and as resources and activities multiplied. But some additions have cluttered up the governmental homestead as lean-tos or as entirely unattached structures, unintegrated and difficult of access.

Additions to the main structure require little attention here, since everyone knows the central points of entrance to them. The responsible citizen, as a general thing, does not need to know the names of particular bureaus in the Defense establishment, the Treasury, Post Office, Justice, and other basic departments in the three primary levels of government. The pathway to them is clear, and the persons to hold responsible for what they do are readily identifiable and subject to punishment or eviction if the public becomes dissatisfied with them.

But there are numerous unintegrated corporations, authorities, districts, and commissions about which the citizen knows little and over which he has little real chance of exercising his sovereign powers. Such organizations have been established at all levels of government and between states and other jurisdictions. Among them there are many different degrees of remoteness from any effective popular control. When they are free from other bad features—and this is by no means always the case—they serve particular interests or aspects of life with almost complete disregard for all others. They normally have only one very special mission, and they are structurally out of touch with and unmindful of other governmental concerns.

This tends to be the case when one or more of these factors can be identified: the groups in highest position in such entities have long-term appointments; their officials cannot be removed by the chief executive of the jurisdiction in which they operate; the agencies have independent revenue resources; they have requirements of excessively legalistic, impersonalized procedures; or they have individual leadership by some inflated personality, a newspaper hero who is an untouchable "prima donna."

Government Independent of Government

The most flagrantly disorganized and least complained about development of this general kind has taken place in the areas of state and local government. A Bureau of the Census study in 1952 listed 116,743 "governments" in the United States, one national, and all of the rest state, interstate, or local. A government as defined in that study is "an organized entity having governmental attributes and sufficient discretion in the management of its own affairs to distinguish it as separate from the administrative structure of any other unit." Some of the characteristics taken as evidence of the three essential attributes—organized entity, governmental character, and substantial autonomy—are perpetual character, right to acquire and dispose of property, officers popularly elected or appointed by public officials, power to levy taxes, to borrow money, to determine budget and fix charges without review by another government.

The 1952 total had been reduced by 38,373, from a total of 155,116 in 1942. One county had been eliminated in the decade, although there remained over 700 with fewer inhabitants than

10,000, of which 252 had less than 5,000 and 14 did not have even 1,000 inhabitants. Aside from that one county, the reduction in jurisdictions had been wholly in number of school boards, which dropped from 108,579 to 67,346, and in townships, which decreased from 18,919 to 17,202. While the school boards decreased numerically, they grew in size and independence.

It is evident that as citizens move from place to place they become involved in different legal and jurisdictional patterns. This tends to be confusing. The very number of jurisdictions is also more confusing than a small number of large and unified institutions whose top officials can be held responsible for everything. Application of the federal theory, emphasis on separation of powers, and a proliferation of unco-ordinated jurisdictions combine to confuse citizens and impair their capacity to perform sovereign functions. Indeed, many of the special state, interstate, and local districts just enumerated, the so-called independent agencies designed to regulate important economic interests at the national level, the Federal Reserve System, and the bank-type structures ostensibly under the Farm Credit Administration were designed and developed, because of special interests or claims to competence, to make general citizen control remote or unreal in any effective way.

The Reserve System is basically banker controlled; it is self-financing, therefore not dependent on congressional appropriations, and is not subject to any systematic executive review. Appointees to the Federal Reserve Board have such long tenure, have in particular instances such confining eligibility requirements, and are so influenced by the still less governmental district boards as to be co-operative with any national administration only at their own rare pleasure. Wholly inconsistent attitudes and actions on the parts of the government and the Federal Reserve Board are by no means unknown, even to the public. A somewhat similar structure was provided for the Federal Land Banks and kindred agencies sheltered under the Farm Credit Administration tent.

Wholly independent special districts, levying charges akin to taxes, expend hundreds of millions a year in various state and local jurisdictions, carrying on important public activities without any real public responsibility or accountability. In New York State a legislative commission reported that as of December 31, 1954, special authorities had total assets of two and one-third billions of dollars; excluding the interests of others in interstate and international authorities, the commission estimated New York's equity at slightly more than two billions. By 1960, this equity was probably more than three billions.

Even such special commissions as that one in New York State find it very difficult to become moderately well informed about these independent agencies, and the legislative commission is at best a spasmodic device for exercising popular control of public agencies. The more revealing information—about the way in which key persons are put on two or more payrolls, the way purchases, contracts, and personal service arrangements with powerful firms and individuals bulwark the independence of these agencies—is not systematically available.

The authorities constitute special power centers within the governmental area, uncoordinated and capable of serving some needs of special publics extravagantly while other needs may be treated stingily by the parent government. It is not strange that most citizens could not guess how many jurisdictions operate in their name, to say nothing of describing their functions and appraising their performance.

The most widespread and numerous of these local "governments" are, of course, school districts. Educators are by no means alone in wanting to be autonomous; it is a common inclination which is basically as irresponsible, even tending to the authoritarian, as it is parochial. Professional foresters have been known to assert that no one has a right to be president unless he is a forester. Lawyers, economists, and businessmen have voiced similar claims for their own kind. Often the movement is to avoid popular control, but it is nominally based on a plea to take a particular function "out of politics." It succeeds because of the general failure to connect popular sovereignty and politics. Nowhere is this plea more persuasive than in defense of educational autonomy.

Usually, school board members are at least subject to the general franchise and have terms of moderate length. But when they are organically dissociated from general government and possessed of independent taxing powers, the schools must be co-ordinated with other public functions in the minds and acts of citizens. The citizens have no official agents charged with responsibility to relate educational expenditures and arrangements to other public undertakings.

The proliferation of autonomous agencies and officials is one of the principal factors in adding to the burdens of sovereign citizens. There are other arrangements that are similarly confusing. Members of governors' cabinets are not usually appointed by the governors to the extent that has been true of presidents' cabinets from the time of our beginning. Some state department heads are chosen by boards largely autonomous, and many others are elected, some in off-year elections when the tendency is greatest to choose persons from the party in opposition to the incumbent governor. These arrangements all becloud responsibility and leave to citizens particular appraisals of performance beyond their reach.

Grants-in-Aid

Grants-in-aid, by the national government to the states, or to the states for local distribution, or directly to local units of government—as for airports, and grants-in-aid from the state itself to cities, counties, towns, and school boards, have become so much a part of the pattern of American government as to be regarded as organic. The objectives of equalization of opportunity of children for education, adequate nutrition, and health services are implicit in democracy, explicit as these benefits become feasible. Similarly, care of the aged and the indigent has a long history, and gives rise to new programs as knowledge and resources are increased. Programs given national aid vary according to differences in state policies, however.

If aid is to be extended for purposes of equalization, it is desirable to know how resources and outlays in the subordinate jurisdictions do and should compare. This is all extremely complicated because of physical differences, population distribution, differences in social conditions, kinds of taxes and methods of assessment.

Where revenues are derived from a variety of sources, however, the problem is even more difficult. In general it may be said, too, that each kind of program requires a different kind of allocation schedule. A national road system arrangement, for example, needs to allow for differences in area and for such facts as that, other elements being equal, road construction costs more per mile in a mountainous state than in a prairie state, more in metropolitan than in rural areas.

These very technical difficulties magnify a confusion that would be inherent in the aid system in any case. In a program in which local, state, and national funds are mingled to serve a common purpose, citizens can hardly be sure whom to praise or blame for what—unless the aid program is new and the same party should be at the particular time dominant in all three levels of government.

For one example, county farm agents are privileged to use United States Department of Agriculture envelopes and mail privileges; on this account they are generally thought of as employees of that department. While they are, or can be, members of the United States government employees' retirement system, they are on no United States payroll, and cannot be hired or fired by any national official. In all states they are paid from national, state, and county funds; in a half-dozen states a single *private* farm organization—the Farm Bureau Federation—is concurrently an employer and a source of funds.

For one more example, that form of social security which provides Old Age and Survivors Insurance is nationally administered; the form that provides unemployment benefits is administered through the states. Administrative costs of the second program vary enormously from state to state, for no good reason that has been discovered, and there is little that any reviewing power has found to do about it.

The Courts

Leaving grants-in-aid, we turn to another area of government in which popular control is limited, but for rather different reasons. This is the field of the courts. National judges are appointed by the president incumbent at the time the vacancy occurs, "by and with the advice and consent of the Senate." They hold office for life, or, with ten years of service, may retire at the age of seventy. There have been very few occasions when a single president might have named a majority, although Washington did it, of course, at the very beginning. The life tenure of judges, the special and jealous support of the legal profession, the nature of the function, and multiple membership in the judicial groups have been among the factors making the national courts generally, and the Supreme Court in particular, highly independent and protected from partisan, even popular, influences.

In the states the judicial pattern is not one but many. Sometimes the judges are outright selections of parties. Sometimes, though party nominees, they are first of all nominees of bar associations or of particular, influential attorneys. In other cases the formal appearance, and sometimes the reality, is some sort of bipartisanship. Nearly always, partly through the influence of the lawyers who are looked to as the pre-eminent authorities on not only juridical but all other matters governmental, there is an aura of untouchability associated with an attribution of holiness. The press reserves for the courts the only constant respect it seems to accord governmental agencies.

In Britain of long ago, antecedent courts were a principal executive arm of the monarch. We find occasional remnants of the ancient system in "county courts," which are not courts as we now use the term, but executive agencies, with coexisting "courts of justice" bearing somewhat different names. In India since independence the "district collector," who for many decades had been tax gatherer, police chief, and magistrate, has been giving up his magistrate functions. Looking at it somewhat differently, one might better say that the magistrate is being compelled to give up control of the police, revenue raising, and general administration. As the courts have been made untouchable and garlanded with haloes, their functions have been confined by other legislative arrangements for administration and, in addition, not infrequently in recent decades, by their own ordinances of self-denial. Such confinement is important in any area of government wherein direct popular control is made difficult.

These governmental areas insulated against normal political

scrutiny, criticism, and control are those where most shocking scandals seem to appear after long periods of inattention. The studies of Sayre and Kaufman in New York City, referred to in Chapter II, seem to suggest that the sale of judgeships is the most frequent impropriety to be found there. Other less formal studies at various times have indicated the same thing to be true in other states, New Jersey and Ohio among them. One sage and seasoned observer of American government, indeed, has asserted to me in conversation that as the executive and legislative branches have been cleaned up corruption has become relatively more frequent in the judicial and "independent agency" fields than in all other parts of government.

The point here is not to assert a judgment of official actions, but to indicate large and important areas of government which in efforts to get functions "out of politics" have been taken out of reach of public control. This is carrying the "check and balance" idea to the point of a blank check and governmental imbalance.

Control Systems

The operational structures most important to the citizen-sovereigns, as with organic structural elements just discussed, have to do with the maintenance of a hierarchical system of control which makes each higher level of responsibility manageable. When sufficiently concerned and agreed, the public must be able to control the legislature and chief executive; both of them, in turn, when convinced of public need or requirement, must in their respective ways be able to control any and all heads of departments and agencies; these heads similarly must be able to control bureau chiefs, who must in turn be able to control division heads, and so on down the hierarchical line.

In no case will control be constant or fully coextensive with function. Everyone in the structure will feel burdened with discretion, as well as surrounded by other people and other functions which must be deferred to. Everyone possessing control powers will exercise them as rarely as possible, with restraint, consideration, and respect for the knowledge and responsibilities of subordinates. Delegation will be general, responsibility will be widely shared. But at each level of responsibility the existence of the capacity to intervene in, modify, or reverse subordinate action in any particular, or in terms of general direction, must be real and unquestioned. Only in some such unbroken structure of relationships is citizen sovereignty conceivable, and it is essential to the citizen function that it be maintained.

The growing complexity of knowledge and functions underscores earlier tendencies to defer too much to experts, and to put persons, because they are experts, into positions where the most serious need is for qualities of general judgment. This tendency is greatest when the experts wear star-spangled uniforms; valid concern for national defense combines with recognition of technical considerations, awe of rank, and perhaps heroic record, to paralyze critical faculties. In lieu of uniform, some services benefit by a mystical or ectoplasmic and gilded halo surrounding the very name of the particular service. Thus too many career members of the Foreign Service are given ministerial and ambassadorial posts, whereas the effort should be to get more and better political appointees. The best heads of diplomatic missions are men of affairs whose economic and political security, as well as personal aplomb, enable them to act more impressively than those who must protect careers. Bunker, Cooper, Bowles, Harriman, Winant—all political diplomats—were all more effective in top posts than any of the dozens of good and able career men I have seen in the same or similar positions.

The quality of the Foreign Service is extremely high in terms of character and intelligence. It has been at its best in recent years when special conditions—notably the war and expansion to handle new programs—caused diversification of membership. In this period there was considerable recruitment of more mature persons, persons with more worldly experience, and with more intimate acquaintance with our own government, than would result from normal recruitment practices. But important ministerial and ambassadorial posts need well-selected political appointees. In diplomacy as in other areas, the old dictum is valid: "Experts should be on tap, not on top."

VI

Every Man a King

MANY CITIZENS have been thoughtful enough about government to recognize that they are not burdened by subjection and regimentation. Yet many such conscientious citizens entertain feelings of near-impotence in the role of sovereign. When every man is a king and every woman a queen the fact of multiple sovereignty dims the legendary glitter of royalty.

The citizen's vote is only one of many, and in most elections his individual abstention would not in fact have changed the immediately identifiable results. The choices open to him in an election, appearing in terms of very numerous individual candidacies against a background of very numerous public issues and problems, seem inadequate, unclear, and inconclusive.

The good citizen is not only impressed with the great number of public problems. The better equipped the citizen is, the more sensitive he is to the highly complicated character of many public issues and the complexity of them in relationship to each other. Feeling rather helpless before the issues and candidacies, he is made to doubt that democracy is real, and to feel that a few high officials, or even some persons wholly unknown to him, are actually making all of the important decisions.

The frustrated sovereigns have often been disposed to blame politics and politicians for everything about government that is

62

unsatisfactory. It is commonly asserted not only that the individual vote means little, but that "all politicians lie," that "political platforms and campaign promises don't mean anything," "politicians prefer to do favors for their friends to serving the general citizen interest," and that "politicians pick candidates they think most likely to win rather than the ones they think would be the best officials."

We cannot have it both ways. If politicians pick candidates most likely to win we can hardly maintain that they are not trying to do what the citizens like. And if political figures and honor are strangers to each other, we are not wholly free from blame if it is clear that the political managers try to pick those who will get our votes. Actually, we have damaged the most important instrument of popular sovereignty by holding politics in contempt, espousing "independent voting" as the only proper practice for self-respecting citizens, and forcing parties to look for financial support in the wrong places. The party function will be further discussed in a later chapter. In this one we are concerned about exploring the general situation of sovereign citizens in a popular government. To what extent should we expect to exert influence, and by what means? And first of all, is the ballot important?

Effectiveness of the Ballot

It is true that sometimes a voter is not able to make up his mind. While if he understood political matters more fully he might come to a decision, so long as he does not it surely is no high crime to withhold his vote. For citizens generally to be able to vote is more essential to the reality of popular government than a 100 per cent turnout. But indecision is only one of many factors reducing the number of voters. Registration difficulties, poll taxes in some states, racial discrimination, absence of adequate arrangements for absentee voting, too long residence requirements in particular jurisdictions, lack of transportation to the polls, and the disfranchisement of residents of the District of Columbia—all of these things have not only made vote totals smaller than otherwise they would have been; all of them reduce ability to vote and therefore impair popular sovereignty. These things are much more serious than withholding votes for want of a definite preference.

Failure of legislative bodies and courts to treat primary elections as true elections has been a handicap to the perfecting of the popular franchise. The way primaries are conducted, and participation in them, should certainly be governed by law as are general elections.

National primary elections for the selection of presidential nominees, however, would be impracticable and highly undesirable. Such primaries would have to be simultaneous to be fair, and this would entail the loss of opportunity for voters to appraise candidates in successive trial heats. If the primary should actually nominate, voters in general would be deprived of the special contributions to the process of selection that the relatively more experienced party leaders now provide in the stressful interplay of national party conventions. The education of party leaders and the exercise of a certain national party discipline now achieved through the national conventions would also be lost.

Further, primaries diminish in usefulness with the number of aspirants to be voted upon. We need greatly to increase both the number and the quality of presidential possibilities, but with even as many as three in the running the likelihood that agreement could be worked out by party members in voting booths all across the country is fantastically remote. The probability—almost the certainty—is that state delegations would be instructed so variously that the parties would be made impotent if the instructions were regarded as at all binding. In the end, nomination would have to be made in a national assemblage in which there was much room for give and take, for negotiation, and for preliminary testing of the intensity of support accorded to particular aspirants. This would put us back where we are now, but somewhat the worse for wear.

Maintenance of presidential primaries in a small number of states, however, helps to educate candidates and helps to provide one basis of popular evaluation of them. Demonstration of vote-getting ability in a national dimension is highly important.

State and local primary elections can serve some good purposes if they are not too invariably mandatory and if they are sufficiently protected by law. They are susceptible to rigging—as when extra, less-than-serious candidacies so split the vote as to throw victory where it would not have gone in a field of serious contenders. Cross-voting—whereby Republicans may vote in Democratic primaries, and Democrats may vote in the Republican ones—should be outlawed. The prohibition of cross-filing—whereby candidates run on more than one party ticket or in more than one party primary—can be readily enforced whenever citizens are sufficiently aroused to demand remedial action. Nomination of candidates carrying a majority of voting districts rather than those receiving a majority of individual votes should also be made unlawful everywhere. But even with all these safeguards, the essential functions of parties can be damaged by too rigid use of primaries. The party should have an underlying and overriding power in all jurisdictions.

At the national level, one of the forms inadequate party discipline takes is confined to a few southern states whose laws permit presidential electors to vote for someone other than the official nominee of the national party. This defect is subject to remedy by either the national conventions or the Congress. Its continuance is an invitation to minority government.

The excessive tendency of voters to try to pick personalities, instead of selecting a party to support, similarly impairs the popular franchise. This is so because it leaves the voter unable to fix responsibility clearly and at the same time confronts him with more choices than he can make sensibly. While the parties themselves do and should pay great attention to personalities, the citizen should either select a *body of personalities* constituting a party offering or should reinforce support of a particular personality at the head of a ticket by voting generally for the ticket he heads.

Yet in spite of all the present imperfections and dubious practices, voting is a better tool of citizenship than many citizens are inclined to believe.

It is true that the margin of victory for particular candidates and party tickets is often so wide that the absence of any single vote would not be of immediately observable significance. Yet if many individuals abstained because of this consideration, the effect would be highly injurious to them and to popular government. Further, single votes count directly in a good many important ways.

The change of a single vote in each election district in New York State, for example, would have lost the governorship for Averell Harriman in 1954. There have been a good many instances in single-party counties in which failure to nominate county tickets with no chance to win locally resulted in loss of the state for the party presidential candidate. Having a ticket in a county of that sort takes a few partisans and friends to the polls who otherwise would have stayed at home, and this activity may affect the outcome of both immediate and later elections.

There are numerous recounts and contests of close elections, and all these emphasize the importance of a few votes that made the determining difference. There are other elections in which a few thousand abstentions or a few hundred shifts in votes from one candidate to another would reverse the results. One such instance importantly affecting the course of history was the election of Franklin D. Roosevelt as governor of New York in 1928 when his predecessor in that office, Alfred E. Smith, failed to carry the state in his race for the Presidency. If Roosevelt's narrow victory had been a defeat it can hardly be doubted that he never would have been president.

Citizen Influence

More constantly, however, the greatest impact of the single citizen on elections is attributable to the fact that a good many individual voters will, spontaneously, act in concert. The single citizen thus becomes a *participant* in a decisive popular movement. That the margin is wide or narrow is itself often an important factor of influence on subsequent administrations. The single voter shares with fellow citizens the ability to swell, retard, or reverse political tides. That in one event the margin was wide in one direction and in the next election favored the opposition proves rather than denies the importance of the individual citizens who produced these results.

Because these popular tides can be created by individuals, officials and potential candidates are enormously sensitive to concerns clearly exhibited and deeply felt. Of course, politicians are generally much more expert than pollsters in appraising the intensity of sentiments, their relative importance in the context of other problems and alternative leaderships, and their transient or lasting character. They are also skillful in distinguishing between some expressions pitched in abstract terms and others that are stated specifically. Most of the time most general positions yield to particular ones, as when belief in a balanced budget gives way readily to belief in the need to strengthen national defense. Politicians know also that citizens quite properly tend to judge entire administrations as a whole, with particular preferences contributing variously to a general judgment. This general judgment is heavily slanted also by a general party preference, to which it is closely akin.

Intensity of attention given to sentiment of citizens does vary somewhat according to the periodicity of official terms. Senators, for example, tend to be more free-wheeling when beginning a six-year term than in the last years of the term. But there is far greater constancy in the ear-to-ground posture than most citizens are inclined to believe. There are differences in wavelengths to which politicians are tuned—differences in whom they know and listen to. These differences are recognizable by citizens, and should be significant to them in choosing candidates and parties.

Because the popular franchise exists, conversations between elections at the dinner party, in the taxicab, in the beauty parlor, at the beach, in stores, offices, and clubs, among faculty members, farm organization members, union members, and over the back fence—all these have a mighty influence. They determine the political climate of the nation and jurisdiction.

While the influence of any single citizen is far from compelling, this is as it should be. No individual judgment can be truly a formulation of "public judgment." Public judgment can only be educed from, or under the discipline of, society at large, through a systematic process of responsible and representative interaction. Public judgment, public policy, and public ethics can properly be formulated only through the brokerage of politicians and the institutional operations of agencies especially equipped for and assigned to special responsibility for the task.

Citizens can freely exercise their responsibilities and rights in a multiple sovereignty given the following:

1. equality in the franchise
2. freedom to criticize and agitate
3. elections never more than a few years apart
4. a secret ballot
5. a two-party system or something approximate to it
6. primaries open only to party members
7. a short ballot
8. an essentially unified governmental structure

Any impairment of these elements calls for vigilance and may require reform. But beyond provision of these essentials, the sovereigns need to proceed in the knowledge that decision on most things that government must attend to can only be achieved in terms of consent, and not in terms of consensus. This should be satisfactory; its realization should diminish the citizen's sense of frustration and point toward effective government as well as pointing the way to proper oversight of the government.

Government by consent includes government action amended under criticism. Indeed, this is one of the most important resources of popular government. Responsible officials would be disposed to delay necessary actions to the great detriment of the country if they did not know that nearly all their decisions could be modified in the light of experience and popular reaction.

Given the basic features listed above, and the conditions then surrounding and limiting official action, decisions made are acceptable as made originally, or become acceptable because of modification, with almost unbelievable regularity.

The structural and procedural factors mentioned all center on the franchise. They are necessary to popular character in one respect in order to provide citizens with the sanctions of sovereignty; in another respect they are needed in order so to fix official responsibility as to make administration accountable by identifying targets for the sanctions. Citizens are by no means so equipped uniformly now in all jurisdictions, and not completely so equipped in any. The most grievous failures are in many local governmental jurisdictions and in some of the states. Because the nation is as large and diverse as it is, the distribution of some of the area shortcomings causes them to cancel each other out, so that the character of the national government must be regarded as much closer to the generally idealized model than many of its subordinate and contributory jurisdictions.

All in all, government in the United States is more completely and variously open to citizen influence and oversight than any other government of anything like comparable scope and complexity. It is not at all certain that sovereign performance is equally outstanding. Certainly there is need among citizens for more understanding of the way in which their governmental institutions do and should perform, and more understanding about how to oversee that performance in ways advancing national welfare and lengthening national expectancy.

Officials Are Frustrated, Too

The more fully the specifications itemized in the preceding section are maintained, the more do officials share in the frustration which citizens often express. Officials are hemmed in to some extent even in nondemocratic institutions. It was widely believed, for example, and it could have been a warranted belief, that at the time of the famous U-2 debacle the dictator Khrushchev acted as he did at the international "summit" in 1960 as a response to his own followerships in and out of the Soviet Union. The forces restraining him are simpler than those having impact on our president. They are simpler in that there are fewer and less systematic but potentially more violent political processes in the Soviet Union than in the United States. His are political restraints, however, and they do make dictatorial powers less than the exaggerated term "absolute" would suggest. But the frustrations of even top officials in democratic governments are enormously more constant, complex, and confining, as well as much more popular in source.

The first duty of government is to avoid disorder. Stated positively, this duty is to make tolerable, sensible, and complementary a host of other-directed interests and activities. Within the government itself, this entails a kind of government by consent achieved by an enormous amount of consultation, coordination, and give-and-take.

Officials superior in rank accept recommendations of subordinate officials and in many matters consent to their decisions. Any decision of the subordinates is a group product in which the result takes account of many different points of view, functions, and responsibilities of other persons in other units and agencies. All these persons, in turn, speak and argue as they do because of at least indirect exposure to many citizens of diverse interests. The whole process takes place under the discipline of a controlling leadership directly responsible to the general public. This leadership can overrule or later modify subordinate decisions, and has sanctions with which to embarrass or punish subordinates who have erred.

The very decision involved has to do in most cases with a drive that has originated in the public scene. Both the legislature and the executive bureaucracy, the former in broader terms than the latter, are charged with formulating responses to citizen expressions of need. The formulations are efforts to answer them, to take account of other attitudes—perhaps not equally expressed—to consider many problems of a technical sort, and to weigh feasibility. They are efforts also to take account of a future a little more visible to "the government," and more within its scope, than within the purview of private citizens.

The legislature consents, more or less, and with modifications, to proposals of the executive and of the executive bureaucracy; the executive and his subordinate organization consent to the requirements of the legislative branch. Both the legislative and executive branches speak with at least a glance toward the judiciary. When it comes the turn of the courts to speak, there are many references to "legislative intent," and to the "magisterial discretion of the executive." Even the Supreme Court makes its decisions (only on matters brought to it) subject to being effectively overruled in as many as a fourth of the instances by lower national or state courts.

The bureaucracy is made up of many persons representative of the various geographical regions, representative of many different functions, interests, bodies of knowledge, and types of experience. The legislative branch is by definition and fact representative of particular constituencies. The president is uniquely elected by national, popular action. Every official is trying to secure decisions that would be acceptable in view of what he knows, whom he knows, to whom he is responsible, what he is responsible for, what is feasible, and what is wise.

By the time the various individuals, units, sections, divisions, bureaus, departments, staff offices, and branches of government have arrived at a mutually acceptable point of view it is almost certain to be something acceptable to the general public, or at least readily alterable so as to win general acceptance. The search for what will win popular consent has become more and more dominant for those in the national government. At state and local levels the forces are similar, but the effective publics are not often so nearly equivalent to the general public. At all levels it may be said that the effort is to avoid a confusing *mess* of diverse pursuits, ideas, procedures, and judgments by making a *mesh* of things that will be accepted by those who have demonstrated capacity to threaten official status.

In the process nobody, not even a president, feels possessed of great power. Rather, all in public service feel hemmed in. When everybody is a king, everybody is frustrated, too. Democracy is the form of government where everybody, or almost everybody, can influence almost everything a little and nobody is likely to be able to influence much of anything in any way very unacceptable to others.

The chief dangers in democracy are implicit in democracy. They are the dangers of the kind that lead to lynching—for lynching is popularly accepted at the place and time where it is done. Mobs, tides of passion, hate, prejudice, fear, and bitterness can overwhelm us. A swell of sentiment in favor of a "preventive war" is not impossible. A comic-book-reading public may demonstrate a preference for demagogues. A public of persons grossly preoccupied with self-interest may demand policies actually harmful to them. And citizens, whose sources of information about public concerns could not possibly equip them to the same degree as public officials are equipped by governmental resources, can hardly be expected to demonstrate foresight equally capable of insuring our continuing well-being.

Responsibility and High Officials

It is a central thesis of this essay that our governmental structures ought to be such that the whole people can impose its will upon the government in a quite precise way when sufficiently agreed and determined as a result of responsible consideration. It is a part of the thesis that the citizens possessed of such power will always be the focus of great concern on the part of all who serve them in official capacities, but that the citizens must know how to use, to rely upon, and to select the ablest persons available for public service. It is for the citizens to exact devotion, to require great integrity and strength and courage of all who are given leadership responsibility. It is for the citizens to discourage the exaggerated distortion of records and arguments which impoverishes "politics." It is for the citizens to choose general direction of the country. And beyond these things, *it is for the citizens to enact ordinances of self-denial so strong that high officials will know themselves to be clearly vested with responsibility to give to the public a quality of government much better than merely that which would be publicly tolerated.* These are truly sovereign responsibilities.

It has been suggested that assumption of responsibility and better acquaintance with the information appropriate to a decision frequently alters one's point of view. On occasion when I have been consulted about policy statements being drafted by my party when it was out of office I have felt compelled to say, "You will have to abandon that position if you are elected; I'd suggest avoiding it now." But, of course, no matter how experienced we are, there are a great many matters about which an out-party group cannot speak with the assurance that it might wish and the public might expect. Former President Truman has been unusually wise on those occasions when, on being asked to express an opinion, he has answered, "I don't know what I would do. I don't have now the information necessary to a judgment." On other occasions he has spoken too quickly, thinking in terms of old situations, and has had sometimes to recant.

Only a week or two after he had unexpectedly succeeded to the Presidency, Mr. Truman showed a most extraordinary awareness of the way in which one's judgment changes with a change in responsibility. The Budget Bureau forms a part of the president's personal staff, and on the transition from Roosevelt to Truman the Bureau personnel made a careful study of Truman's votes in the Senate and his expressions of opinion in that body, in committee, and elsewhere. The record was assembled in an attractive, leather-covered looseleaf book which Director Harold Smith took to the White House to exhibit as a sign of the Bureau's responsiveness to new leadership. The new President turned over the pages with much nostalgic interest, and at the last page asked if a book of this sort could be made for him. After he was assured that this would be done, he said, "But don't you fellows pay much attention to it; I wasn't president then."

The judgment capable of guiding an organization and making its policies derives in large part, but not exclusively, from the organization itself. If we adopt the reasonable view of Barnard, referred to previously in Chapter IV, that customers are at least momentarily members of the organization from which they buy, we must feel even more positively that the citizens of a democracy are permanent members of their governmental organization. Yet some of the materials of good and relevant judgment will derive from a community larger than any single operating organization even so broadly defined. For the United States government, what can be foreign policy depends to a large extent, and properly, on other nations. Within the United States a body of persons who have never purchased a product of a particular company and perhaps never will is still capable of influencing the climate of opinion to which that company must pay some attention. Much more does sentiment from many quarters get governmental consideration.

Even so, the wisest person not deeply immersed in the affairs of a given organization and not actually responsible to it is not at all likely to be able to produce a judgment directly acceptable to and wise for that organization to adopt literally as proffered. An executive may be an incompetent fool, but the alternative to his decision is not the irrelevant judgment of an irresponsible wise man. The alternative is to bring the wise man in, so expose him as to make his judgment relevant, and make him shoulder responsibility for it. Until that is done the outside observer is moderately useful as a commentator, and he is the unchallengeable authority on what he likes and dislikes, but no more. His judgment is not actually substitutable for that of the present decision-maker until he has personally been substituted for him. In all probability his judgment will not be the same afterwards as it was before he was so substituted.

Citizens Must Delegate

An analogy highly useful to citizens can be drawn between their situation with regard to the president and Congress, the governor and the legislature, and the situation between the president and his cabinet, or the governor and his cabinet. Indeed, it is the next-level-up version of a relationship that exists between department heads and bureau chiefs, bureau chiefs and their division heads, or between any other two levels of an operating institution.

In every one of these relationships the official higher up can do what he needs to do only because he can utilize others, can delegate duties to others. The man at the top must realize that orders issued when applied in many different situations must be applied with flexibility in ways he cannot fully see and could not anticipate. He relies upon the discretion of subordinates for nice adjustments of policy, for important intelligence, for recommendations, for co-ordination with their opposite numbers in other units or agencies having related responsibilities.

A common remark of field employees of the national government to visitors from Washington headquarters is, "You don't know conditions in the field." This is bound to be more or less so. A proper retort is, "And you don't know conditions in Washington," which is also valid. Good administration reconciles or balances the two points of view, and many others.

When subordinates propose courses of action, the higher ranking official often will be justified in accepting them, knowing the special competence of the subordinates, knowing that the proposals have been worked out with the consent of other units and agencies having related responsibilities, and having no alternatives or modifications to propose important enough to justify interference.

The higher the level of responsibility, the more delegation is required, since more work is involved, and since more complications and technical matters must be taken into account. The higher the responsibility, then, the more must power be kept in reserve and used to provide *general* direction, to remedy demonstrated shortcomings, or to exercise initiative and guidance in matters of great importance for which those in the higher level have special capacities because of their vantage points and the nature of their special responsibilities. Delegation is not abdication. It is a way of supervising many activities, and utilizing many abilities.

There are things known "in Washington" not known in the field. It may be wise to insist upon certain things on occasion because of what is discernible only at the higher level. Occasionally, even though the higher position gives no new relevant information, the fact that a greater responsibility is vested there and that the holder of it cannot conscientiously accept what is recommended will justify disapproval or modification. Much more often, after a course of action has been tried with unsatisfactory results, change must be directed from the higher level.

This is the nature of delegation, and delegation there must be in all large affairs, more and more of it in higher and higher places of responsibility. The institutions of popular government place citizens in the very highest level—that of sovereigns—in the organization having the most transactions involving more considerations than any other. The citizen sovereigns can achieve governance, can uphold their high responsibilities, only by utilizing others of the greatest competence attainable. Each citizen needs to know how to delegate, how to give oversight appropriate to his sovereign status rather than merely in terms of his simple interests as a subject of the government.

The requirements partake of top-level administration. The guides to administrative excellence include these: Do not make decisions others should make; do not be panicked or pressured into premature decision; remember that the higher the level of responsibility, the more general should be the nature of decisions;

remember that the prerequisite to enforcing a policy change usually is identification and consideration of an actual alternative.

For popular decision-making to be manageable, these guides suggest not trying to make too many decisions, and concentrating heavily on the decisions that have to be made in elections, in which there are definite alternatives in two-party jurisdictions, posing a choice between two possible administrations.

The most broadly effective administrative decisions are almost always those involving "personnel." Experienced administrators coming into a gubernatorial post or into the Presidency have been known to say, "The appointments I make now will make or break me; when I have made them I become the prisoner of my own appointees."

Whether or not to change administrations and parties is the equivalent decision available to sovereign citizens, and things that indicate what kind of appointments will be made by the chief executive elected should be important factors in arriving at a judgment. That a Republican will appropriately appoint Republicans, as a Democrat will appoint Democrats, is a major indication of what choice voters should make. The environing influence the known leaders of the Republican party would have on a Republican president may be meaningfully compared with the kind of influence Democratic leaders would exert on a Democratic president.

By way of illustrating this point, it may be remarked that Mr. Eisenhower, after a long and distinguished military career, would choose some appointees from the defense field where there were friends in whom he had confidence. Yet he would be inclined to think he knew all the answers to problems in the military field, while he tended to be in awe of big business men and to take too seriously their advice after appointing them to high posts. Mr. Truman, as an old party hand, understood thoroughly the political nature of his office, worked happily with Dean Acheson who could discuss history, but as an old field-artillery captain he tended to be awed by General Marshall.

Citizens can do more to live up to their sovereign responsibility by selecting for nominees to chief executive posts in state and nation the ablest political executives available in their respective parties as candidates, and by maintaining membership in the party whose general record, attitudes, and leadership are most attractive. They should avoid yes-men as they would avoid personal bankruptcy. They should look for strong men, of courage and high integrity, men who can lead, men whose competence has been developed in long political apprenticeship, in a good many elective campaigns, and in executive posts politically responsible. They should look for action-oriented men, intelligent men, but men who understand the limitations of logic. They should avoid the merely agreeable, the Hollywood starlet, the bright boy, the David Harum type whose skill is horse trading or mediation rather than leadership. For nomination to legislative posts executive qualities are not necessary in most cases, but other requirements should be high.

So we return to the problem of leadership equal to our sovereign aspirations. The leadership we need will not always happen to appear in the right place at the crucial moment. We need to select the best available at all times. We need also to enrich the resources of availables. Identification of competent leaders and development of more potential leaders of high ability is the noblest task of citizens concerned to exercise their sovereignty.

VII

Choosing Official Leaders

PERSONNEL OFFICES, top executives, and boards of directors find nothing more difficult, nothing more worthy of careful and extensive methods, than the identification and development of important appointees and administrative internes from among whom will be found top officers in later years. Selections for posts of high importance are extremely hard to make with confidence. For even more compelling reasons, the most important and difficult tasks of sovereign citizens are the choices of parties and candidates to be vested with the crucial responsibilities of governance for particular periods.

For presidents and governors, the appointments of department and agency heads are largely determining of entire administrations. A vote for a Republican chief executive is a vote for Republican department and agency heads; a vote for a Democrat is a vote for Democratic department and agency heads. A general election is primarily a choice of "administrations"—a choice of party. Citizen participation in choice of individual officials is essentially an intraparty activity.

Parties are basically state and local organizations. The character of a party and of political issues between the parties consequently extends more consistently through all the levels of government than many voters usually recognize. Discussion of the choice of nominees of any level is therefore in a degree relevant to all levels. Partly for this reason, and also because of the vividness of the highest office, discussion of the choice of nominees here may focus chiefly on the Presidency. Conditions that make it difficult to secure suitable state and local officials also limit the supply of presidential possibilities. Rigors of controversy and attack, uncertainty of tenure, and inadequacy of party and personal financing discourage innumerable candidacies, affecting all levels of government.

Philip Willkie, a banker from Rushville, Indiana, while serving in his state legislature told me that eight members of that body, all abler, he thought, than the best of the Indiana congressional delegation, would quit politics at the end of the term they were then serving. They felt that they had done as much of their bit as they could afford.

Another condition which inhibits the development of political leadership limits politics at its supposedly most pristine grassroots. The young lawyer who hangs out his shingle in a small county-seat town may frequently—even unconsciously—decide to be a Republican in a one-party Republican county, or a Democrat in a one-party Democratic jurisdiction, because the way to advertise himself and build a future career is to be elected county attorney. In the past, at least, the weekly newspaper publisher, often somewhat similarly determined his party affiliation in most states with a view to getting "county printing." Economic interest and concern about status combine to stimulate a drift toward association with the established majority.

Short of some kind of political or social earthquake, therefore, a one-party jurisdiction tends to become steadily more firmly petrified, leadership less significantly contested. There is often in such conditions, too, a kind of bossism less subject to legitimate popular influences than are political machines in cosmopolitan cities. In the smaller, one-party community, the boss frequently is the most skillful and inveterate political lawyer, long past the county-attorney stage. The boss often has as his key associates the party newspaper publisher and a leading banker who holds the notes of many citizens. The lawyer must be seen by any citizen before officials at the courthouse will act with regard to the sale of tax-delinquent property and many another bit of business which should require only official attention.

These and many other practices diminish and defile the primary sources of political leadership. The short supply of promising material at state and local levels is related to the serious lack of adequate material at the national level. The problem there was succinctly pointed up by Henry Steele Commager in an article in the *New York Times Magazine* of January 17, 1960:

> The United States of the Seventeen Seventies and Eighties was a new nation on the frontier of civilization, with a population of some three million (far less than that of Los Angeles County today) spread thin over an immense territory, without a single real city, without an aristocracy or a ruling class, and with few of those institutions of science and learning that sustained the societies of the Old World. Yet out of this America emerged, in a single generation, Washington, Franklin, Jefferson, Hamilton, John Adams, James Wilson, John Jay, James Madison, John Marshall and a score of others scarcely less distinguished in the realm of statesmanship.
>
> Now we have everything that we then lacked. Our population is fifty times as large as that of 1780, our territory spreads across the continent, we count a hundred cities larger than the largest of that time, we boast an educational level higher than any other in the Western world, as well as immense wealth and power. We have, in fact, all the elements that should produce statesmen. Yet in the past half century we have produced perhaps three men comparable to those of the Revolutionary generation.

A more detailed examination and discussion of our leadership record may help explain why a society otherwise so affluent is so poverty stricken in terms of political leadership. It may even hint at ways to better our condition.

Rating Presidential Leadership

Amplifying Commager's statement somewhat, we may say that during the first fifty-two years of our history we had eight presidents, seven of whom should be rated from "adequate" to "strong," the eighth something a bit better than mediocre. In the sixty succeeding years extending to the turn of the century—about the same as the last period to which Commager conceded three strong presidents—there were three adequate-to-strong presidents. Thirteen other men served as president during this period, but three held office for too short a time to be evaluated, and four had succeeded to the office by the death of a president without themselves ever having been elected to the top office. Because of mortality and the relative inattention given to choice of vice-presidential nominees, if for no other reasons, these seven can all be rated as only "mediocre." Five men elected to the Presidency served out their terms and still must be rated as "mediocre or worse."

The record, then, is a series of adequate presidents in the first half-century, only three adequate or better ones in the next sixty years, and only three or four adequate or better in the next sixty-year period. For reasons of whatever circumstances, out of thirty-three different men who before 1960 had occupied the highest office at our bestowal, we have had only thirteen or fourteen adequate presidents, half of them at the very beginning of our political history. About 27 per cent of our presidents since Jackson might be rated as adequate or better, while their years in service have comprised 40 per cent of that time period.

Certainly one of the chief reasons for the decline after Jackson is to be found in the transition from a founding to a going-concern situation. Our brilliant group of founding figures developed out of a society enormously concerned about government, in which there was an assumption by the ablest men of the time of a compelling responsibility for the building and servicing of new and superior governmental institutions. Nowadays the patterns of basic interest set for our young people are extremely different, resulting in a wide disinterest in public service and much hostility to government.

The Founding Fathers were generally so situated economically that they could devote major attention to governmental matters, and at the same time so dedicated, so stirred, that they did this with great unselfishness and idealism. The idealism was hard-

headed, for these were men of substantial affairs. Most large operations of that day were agricultural. (Washington, as the
extreme example, owned 110,000 acres of land.) The situation
was such that the first eleven to occupy the presidential office
were men of affairs as broad and diverse as the country afforded,
including practically lifelong and deep involvement in political
matters. The devising, establishing, and early direction of the
nation were in the hands of men with extraordinary managerial
and political preparation.

Even after the early concentration of abilities and energies on
the handling of public affairs, some features of a pattern were
more or less maintained. All but five presidents had prior
elective political experience, most of them a great deal of it,
frequently in two levels of government and a few in all three
levels. Of the five with no elective experience, two—Taft and
Hoover—had served in appointive posts. The other three—Taylor,
Grant, and Eisenhower—were professional military men. All
other presidents with military experience were temporary or
emergency soldiers, not professionals.

With one exception, through the administration of Andrew
Johnson, prior political experience of the successive presidents
ranged from twenty-one to forty-two years. The exception was
General Taylor, whose record did not even include voting before
his own nomination for the top office.

Since the Civil War, political experience of men coming to the
White House has been somewhat less, but with five exceptions has
ranged from nineteen years (Theodore Roosevelt, when he succeeded to the office at the age of forty-two) to thirty-four years
(Coolidge). Eisenhower and Grant, as the two professional military men since the Civil War, alone had no political preparation.

Resources for Presidential Leadership

What proportion of our ablest men have had the political
background we have required of our presidents? No one knows,
but it is obviously very small. What proportion have been able
concurrently to gain large and diverse experience with affairs
somewhat representative of the general concerns of our citizens?
The number we might guess must be smaller yet when we raise

this question. When we refine the inquiry further to require at least a few years of political *executive* experience, the number must be reduced again. Not one of the great congressional figures went on to the Presidency—not Clay, or Webster, or Calhoun, as examples—although nearly all presidents have had some legislative experience. Intermittently throughout our history, the elective political record has also included those with experience in the executive branch of government—most frequently through service as a governor.

As already suggested, the financial insecurity of political life requires supplemental resources. More than three-fourths of the men coming to the Presidency have been in comfortable financial circumstances, or even wealthy. If this is a general requirement, it enormously limits actual eligibility. A related factor is the kind of career in which one may earn while working at politics, or may attain a competence quickly. Of the last sixteen presidents, nine were lawyers, three others were men of independent means and no longer dependent upon their earning capacity. For perhaps a majority of men in politics the law offers a road to income built out of activities related to politics even when not related to office-holding. There is a peculiarly American extreme in the close affinity here between the law and politics, and it is by no means altogether salutary. In any case, the field of eligibles is greatly narrowed by such close confinement to a single type of career.

There are other restrictions on eligibility, some of them only conventions and some reflecting shrewd political judgment. Up until 1960 only male Protestants have had the office of president, and they have been drawn from only thirteen of our fifty states. No one has been elected who has not spent at least thirty years in this country. Nearly all presidents have lived in only one state, since elevation by party is first of all a state phenomenon. Except for presidential primaries, which are expensive and in order only late in a career, there is almost no way to campaign in any national sense, or to develop national experience, responsibility, and acquaintance. The people at large have little chance to observe possible nominees over a period of years and are therefore aware of very few potential candidates.

The great number of one-party cities, districts, and states

greatly reduces the number and quality of potential leaders. Real leaders of competence are cultivated in jurisdictions where political competition has more variety and range and where a cosmopolitan body of citizens actively concerned causes the outcome of balloting to be in perennial doubt. It is a sound instinct that causes politicians and other citizens to look to cosmopolitan, volatile, two-party states for national leadership possibilities.

Leadership material is also diminished and demeaned by the outrageous constitutional, legal, and prejudicial barriers to re-election. Many a promising young governor has had no further career for no reason other than that he could not seek a second or a third term. Some, on this account, have been led to seek higher office too soon and have reached limbo by that route. The better way to identify and select leaders is to maintain their eligibility for further development and competition. Re-election should come only on merit, but should not be denied for any other reason.

As a general thing, a politician's effectiveness is largely a product of his situation in a definite post wherein his strictly personal strength is enhanced by status. A man very powerful in the Senate will have much less influence with his former colleagues the moment he accepts another post—even one as an important aide to the president. A former president, or a man once or even twice nominated for the Presidency, has a certain prestige thereafter, but much less ability to affect political action than many observers seem to believe. Indeed, very few persons in or out of office can individually deliver to anybody else much of the support they can secure for themselves, and very few have very great followerships apart from position achieved through party processes. Organizational support is crucial to achievement that is essentially institutional, and such support is largely associated with responsible status.

Because of all these elements holding down the number of the really eligible, and in desperation for lack of demonstrated leadership material, parties may sometimes select a political freshman or an unknown as a "dark horse" nominee for the highest post in the land. In this century the Democrats nominated Alton B. Parker and John W. Davis; the Republicans once chose Alfred E. Landon, who had had only three years in public office, while on another occasion they chose a veritable neophyte, Wendell Willkie. When the latter, much better qualified after his earlier experience and with capacity to learn very quickly, entered the race four years later, he was then limited to the conventional intraparty procedures and could not reach the quarter-pole. These frustrated and frustrating efforts underscore the feeling one gets from surveying the long line of such presidents as Taylor, Tyler, Fillmore, Arthur, Grant, Pierce, Buchanan, and some of their successors. We and our citizen antecedents may have done a pretty good job of selecting the best from among those presidential and vice-presidential possibilities who were actually eligible. But if this is the case, the high proportion of mediocrities surely suggests that our system is not producing nearly enough high-grade eligibles.

Presidential Burdens and "Executive Prerogative"

The need for competent leadership has expanded in keeping with our enlarged view of the universe and our increased command of technologies. At the presidential level the need is now widely recognized to be so great as to justify the most serious and sustained attention. In the perspective of history only the strong presidents are venerated; in the contemplated future, only very strong presidents can be afforded.

It is commonplace to stress the precariousness of civilization before the possibilities of modern warfare. Everyone has been startled and challenged by our forays into space. These things change the everyday content of all governmental responsibilities of any high level. But other developments greatly add to the problems and possibilities. The very growth of population; the shift from a rural to a largely urban society; the spread of great metropolitan complexes intricately interdependent but organically separate; the obsolescence of many representational arrangements; the new learnings that offer health in terms never before imagined, that increase the number of the aged and demand still more learnings and learning facilities; the enlargement of economic resources that open miraculous capacities for enriched welfare and greater human development—all these and many more press hard upon the facilities and the leaders of popular government.

The beginning of sovereign wisdom required to address these new conditions surely is in a fresh consideration of the greatly enhanced significance of the presidential office, its potentialities, and ways in which more constantly we may select more competent presidents from larger fields of qualified eligibles.

The invention of the Presidency was the greatest single product of the Constitutional Convention. The chief executive's individual function is uniquely national in a nation notably pluralistic. Being one person responsible to the whole people, he holds the office that can formulate specific proposals and take specific actions with an expedition and a clarity nowhere else possible in this country.

The crucial significance of the office of the Presidency could not begin fully to appear until recently, when we have seen problems of state attain dimensions and character far beyond the resources of all who are more specially situated, more specially responsible, and less equipped with institutional resources. The soberest among political thinkers have come, consequently, to new respect for the theory of "executive prerogative"—an emphatic version of the conception of "implied powers."

Aside from the change in nature and size of problems, this shift in thought has been stimulated by a great increase in the number of persons intellectually able and inclined to verbalize learnings out of actual experience in and with government. The intellectual shift has been away from an extreme concentration on the history of political ideas developed apart from politics and related to times antedating our own history. In one particular, a new attention has been given to actions of our presidents deviating from their own earlier expressed theories. Jefferson's purchase of the Louisiana Territory through the agency of three great contemporary figures—Madison, Monroe, and Livingston—provides an unparalleled example of a quartet in action meeting a great need and a great opportunity by going contrary to their earlier verbalisms. David S. Muzzey's statement in his book *Thomas Jefferson* (New York: C. Scribner's Sons, 1918) is succinct and drastic:

This advocate of strict economy had spent on his own executive authority an amount equal to almost three-fourths of the debt which Hamilton had assumed for the states with the sanction of Congress. This champion of the letter of the Constitution had exercised the power of acquiring foreign territory and promising foreigners citizenship of the United States, for which no clause could be found among the 'enumerated powers.' This opponent of the extension of the 'general government' had stretched its power far beyond any point the Federalists had reached, and had laid the foundation, in the creation of an immense national territory in the West, for that definitive triumph of the nation over the States which his 'countrymen' Southerners of the second generation fought so desperately to avert.

The friendship of Jefferson with his former political foe, John Adams, in their years of retirement, consequently reflected more than the mellowing of age; it represented a drawing together of Republican and Federalist champions on the basis of a common experience in responsibility. This view is further supported by John Quincy Adams' co-operation and then full association with the party of Jefferson.

Lincoln's practice in managing the nation's pursuit of survival was similarly rooted in "prerogative," and was similarly a reversal, under responsibility, of views earlier expressed. From Washington on, the Presidency has always been, in spite of weaklings, the crucial means through which survival and effectiveness have been found. Hence, as more and more persons of scholarly quality have had official responsibility or come to places where observation of the reality has not been obscured, there has been a movement away from the position in which most theoreticians seemed to assume that not much could be learned from modern experience.

Yet the conception of "executive prerogative" is not a new one. John Locke almost three centuries ago had coupled the necessity for executive power going beyond or contrary to law with any formal division of legislative and executive powers. A passionate believer in popular government, he could be said to have coupled democracy and executive prerogative in what he called "the com-

mon law of nature." He asserted that the limits on him who has
the power and sits without adjournment are not in written docu-
ments. The limits he found in this sentence: "If there comes to
be a question between the executive power and the people about
a thing claimed as a prerogative, the tendency of the exercise of
such prerogative to the good or hurt of the people will easily
decide that question." This he could say only on the assumption
that basic arrangements give to the people power to assert their
sense of "good" or "hurt."

That this has been a gradually emergent view among political
scientists during the last few decades is especially well demonstrated in writings of Clinton W. Rossiter (*The American Presidency*, New York: Harcourt, Brace & Co., 1956), Richard E. Neustadt, and Rowland Egger ("Challenges to Traditional Ethics:
Government, Politics, and Administration," 1960 Conference on
Science, Philosophy and Religion, New York: Harper), ema-
nating from the sober academic halls of Cornell, Columbia, and
Virginia. There also is a new recognition of the existence of more
restraints on presidential power than the important and basic
sanctions directly available to the people in their capacity to evict
or to retain through the franchise. The checks and balances are
enormously greater and more complicated than our forefathers
could have anticipated. The president's institutional dependence
on a very great number of persons with differentiated functions
and responsibilities means, in effect, that even the most "top
secret" business gets vigorous and jealous debate and scrutiny
which constitute a surprisingly representative review.

Neustadt in his extraordinarily informed and wise book (*Presidential Power: The Politics of Leadership*, New York: Columbia
University Press, 1960) itemizes a series of important ways in
which actions we once either regarded as infeasible or treated as
exceptional have been transformed into routine responsibilities
of the president. The Railway Labor Act, the Taft-Hartley Act,
the Employment Act, U.N. membership, alliances, the National
Security Act, and the Atomic Energy Act are tremendous items
putting modern burdens on the Presidency so that acceptance of
the chief executive as the Great Initiator "is as widespread at the
Capitol as in the White House itself." But this "merely signifies

that other men have found it practically impossible to do *their* jobs without assurance of initiatives from him. Service to themselves, not power for the President, has brought them to accept his leadership in form."

Recalling Woodrow Wilson's remark that a president has liberty "to be as big a man as he can," Neustadt says that nowadays he cannot be as small as he might like. He then brilliantly depicts the give-and-take which is the active form of presidential power in a vastly complicated process of interaction of responsibilities, and approvingly quotes Truman's declaration that presidential power is the power to persuade.

It is only in this sense that I can accept his statement that Franklin Roosevelt, "hungry for the Presidency's power as his natural birthright, should exemplify the man who helps himself." (This was followed by a reference to Truman, personally known to Neustadt, who "felt no such hunger and laid claim to no such birthright, yet still created from his background, and his heroes, and his reading, an image of the office that impelled him toward self-help.") I knew Roosevelt as well as Truman. I accept without quibble Neustadt's language about the latter. Roosevelt certainly was not surprised, as Truman was, to find himself in the White House, and he knew from earlier experience the importance of protecting and utilizing his prerogatives. Yet he delegated widely, accommodated persons of quite different political purposes, found it almost impossible to "fire" anyone, was less disposed to assert raw power with each passing day in office, and regarded his principal job as that of an educator.

The point is that we have never had a president who resorted increasingly to use of "power" as commonly understood, because, as one sage civil service observer concluded after forty-two years, "If for no other reason, they find out they can't." It follows also that what the "strong president" strives for is effectiveness in his responsibility—the use of tactics, strategy, negotiation, imagination, give-and-take, and social and political skill for carrying on the affairs for which he has become especially responsible. There is herein a requirement for a special and superb kind of craftsmanship. The final conclusion is that so far as any discerning person can see we shall always hereafter need "strong presidents."

It has been necessary to discuss these general considerations at this length for the very reason that we can no longer be bound so much as we have been heretofore by literal views of our Constitution, our government, and our political leadership. Literal actions are for unchallenged routines and for those incapable of or not needing discretion. What we mean by "statesmanship" requires high discretion. It is not necessary to accept any particular justification for abandoning the old dogmas, or even to deny them all validity—they have even now a limited usefulness in that they require caution and deny the chief executive and all others unlimited license—but it is important to challenge them, to escape from the mortal damage stubborn confinement to them would entail.

The nation must be able to do in the times ahead the great and vital things modernly equivalent to what Jefferson and Lincoln did in their times. No dogma should prevent governmental effectiveness. No weakling in the Presidency should bring failure to the great American aspiration. No competent president should be required to lead us to failure.

Defining the meaning of "governmental adequacy" and "presidential effectiveness" in ever-changing circumstances is the eternal business of popular politics. To try to answer the always different and always emerging problems by invoking certain dogmatic phrases, such as the clichés discussed in earlier chapters, is to evade our sovereign responsibility and to doom our kind of social order to ruin. It is important in considering what kind of men to choose as presidential candidates to see what our history has clearly demonstrated: that those bearing public responsibility in the United States are so hemmed in by the need to utilize and relate and defer to many people, many functions, many interests, and many responsibilities, that we are very much more likely to find these men inadequate than to find them capable of usurpation.

The Search for Qualified Candidates

Turning to specific points citizens might profitably have in mind in regard to the selection of nominees, first emphasis should be given to the fact that at every level the best candidates are scarce; they become rarer in successively higher posts. There is no single formula except the incomplete one which emphasizes the unvarying necessity for prior political experience as nearly as possible commensurate with the office to be filled. Actually, most persons have engaged in activities in addition to being politicians, and the type and quality of this second career is an important consideration. At best, too, it must be admitted that there is not really any possible prior experience available that is nearly commensurate with the Presidency.

It is true, also, that much previous political experience is not conclusive. Those under consideration may have served a certain representational purpose, may somehow have balanced tickets or party elements in a particular jurisdiction, or may have filled in because of the absence of anyone known to be better qualified. In politics as in everything else, the learning of years may be repetitive rather than accumulative.

Our political structure can hardly provide us with candidates for national office who have previously held national elective office and therein exercised national responsibility and demonstrated a national outlook. All elective offices other than that of president are filled at local and state levels. Candidates and party leaders, consequently, are likely to be excessively parochial in outlook prior to an experience in presidential primaries. City "bosses" are important nationally only because of localized power, not because of national or even regional strength or competence. As a large body they may make suitable national nominations in a process of pressurized interaction, but the individual candidates so chosen should have much larger and broader capacities.

Philip Stoddard Brown, able business and financial writer for the *Washington Post*, concluded a brilliant review of a long procession of business men in government by saying, "To be head of a large corporation is not qualification enough for a top government job—or should not be." He was speaking about appointive posts, and his conclusion would be even more emphatic if addressed to the Presidency.

Political professionals are properly influenced by evidence of popular appeal; they wish to nominate candidates who are likely to win. They know that most people are inclined to stand in awe before great business and industrial figures, or to be captivated by some "father figure," some charmer, or someone so much publicized for irrelevant achievements as to be extraordinarily well known. At the local level in particular, the wounded war veteran or the man with a large family or the largest collection of lodge and club memberships may be much too readily accepted. Indeed, the official biographies of some members of Congress recite ridiculous membership details. When the citizens put sufficient emphasis on relevant qualifications the quality and abilities of office holders will be of a much higher order than the past national average.

To be an "egghead" is neither a qualification nor a disqualification; it all depends upon what kind of egghead, in what complex of other attributes. Certainly, high political posts should not go to the oldest citizen or to the one with the highest I.Q. But they require maturity—which may come early in some cases—and very high intelligence, even though not of the sort represented by the professional intellectual. The qualities of mind needed are those that make for quick perception, high power of concentration of attention, keen intuitions, extraordinary social sense, quick selection from fruits of past experience and reflection, readiness to act, along with a poise and judgment which avoid acting or talking too much, too soon, or excitedly.

Such qualities of mind are associated with qualities of heart, stomach, and skin. A tough skin capable of withstanding heavy blows, great physical endurance, a courageous and a sympathetic heart, a stomach for the tussles of politics—these are all highly desirable. They tend to equip a candidate with a capacity for judgment that is as much visceral and intuitive as it is mental. They pertain to such an office as that of president only when they are the qualities of one who also has a general understanding of the whole country and of our government. Even for the handling of foreign policy, this domestic equipment is prerequisite.

Knowing the country involves understanding and having fellow feeling for all manner of people. Most persons, even many who are especially gregarious, are acquainted only in limited circles. Extremely wealthy persons who have never made their own income tax returns nor experienced hardships are much more handicapped in social understanding than they or their admirers usually suspect. Yet political life is more feasible for those with some means, and one with inherited comfort is on the whole more likely to be socially sensitive than the "self-made" man. A millionaire publisher who had made his own fortune once remarked to me after telling me the story of his career, "If two ants are walking on the sidewalk and one is stepped on by a pedestrian, the other ant takes credit for earned success." The self-made man is likely to feel that all others are at fault for not having done as well as he has. He may be where he is because of an especially ruthless character inappropriate to popular leadership. In any case, his preoccupations have had to be far removed from politics.

Successive subjection to electoral tests, varied experience in responsible decision-making processes of public character—these are the means whereby candidates equip themselves for office. Observant and critical citizens should appraise aspirants in light of their performance on these political terms. One who does not consciously and persistently desire public office is most unlikely to be an effective official. One who wants it too much, on the other hand, will not serve well. The primary difference is in the mixture of ambition and skill with dedication.

Thoroughgoing elective experience is the prerequisite to any claims to high office, but the experience should be of a kind, as nearly as may be, which is representative of the whole jurisdiction and as nearly like the office aspired to as possible. Specifically, this means that the winning of elections in a highly homogeneous jurisdiction has little bearing elsewhere. Superior political abilities are required of a winner in a highly cosmopolitan jurisdiction where issues are many, competition keen, the two-party system real. Governors of states answering this description should be more carefully considered for presidential nominations than other governors—provided that constitutionally and in practice the governorship of the particular state is inherently strong. Where heads of state departments are individually elected, not appointed and removable by the governor, and where representational patterns prevent the governor from having appropriate influence on the legislature, the office is not that of a chief executive. There are only a handful of states in which the "strong governor" pattern has been established, and one of these—Virginia—is not yet a politically cosmopolitan state.

New Popular Attitudes

Reviewing the terms on which citizens select nominees for elective office, especially the Presidency, one might assume that the press would be a source of the greatest assistance. Upon examination, however, this assumption is found to be unwarranted. Frank R. Kent, a distinguished journalist of a generation ago, once wrote a blistering indictment of the press as largely responsible for "the continuance in public life of the fakes, frauds, and fools who wield power in our city, state and national governments." Most of all, Kent criticized the press for failure to provide the country with a valid picture of presidents and near-presidents. I intend no such bitter indictment of either officials or press.

It is true, I think, that the soberest commentators require years to arrive at a judgment of performance that politician observers reach in a fraction of the time. I think it also true that the convention of making dramatic situations out of lifeless ones causes reporters to view each political contest as a breathless race, each major contender as one of the great figures of the century—until one loses. But I have tried to imagine how the news columns might be made a vehicle of critical, objective evaluation, and, except in one particular, I have come to conclude that this cannot and should not be done. The particular exception is in the obvious and entirely feasible responsibility of the press to report provable wrongdoing of officials.

The clearest important resource of newspapermen not equally available to citizens at large is personal acquaintance with officials and candidates. It is this which leads the citizens to read the news as implying evaluations not in fact intended or justified. And the principal reform in this instance seems to me to be a responsibility of citizens for a change in their expectations and use of the news. The newspaper writers do what is required of them. Citizens must do for themselves what is a fulfillment of their responsibilities; they would not delegate their responsibilities as voters to the correspondents and commentators.

Evaluation of aspirants for public office is most extensive and complicated when it comes to choosing nominees. After nomination, the choice is between parties. Even insofar as it is still thought of as a choice between individuals it is at that stage limited to two possibilities. The initial and basic evaluation in terms of individual qualifications, then, is a party responsibility and function. The newspaper participating in that function would be properly loyal to a single party. This would entail open recognition of a party affiliation, which many publishers nowadays do not believe advantageous and party organizations might not at all welcome. If carried beyond the editorial page, this assumption of special nomination influence would impair relationships between publishers, editors, and reporters, and would challenge all claims to reportorial objectivity. If not carried beyond the editorials there would be no significant change from present practice. The role of the press in government is discussed more fully in a later chapter.

Citizen judgment can be enriched most of all by an increase in the availability of suitable leadership material. The most feasible changes that might contribute to such an increase are those that are wholly within the control of the voters themselves; these are matters of popular attitudes. Better utilization of Cabinet members and agency heads provides a special example. Politicians would prefer to appoint politicians to such posts, and to deputy positions. But the popular prejudice is strongly insistent upon a farm leader for Secretary of Agriculture, a banker for Secretary of the Treasury, a labor mediator or equivalent for Secretary of Labor, and an industrial tycoon for Secretary of Commerce.

Cabinet and similar officials should be the best substitutes for the nonexisting nationally elected officials below the rank of president. (The Vice-Presidency is not an executive position at all unless a particular incumbent is actually made head of some important program-operating agency. Nor are vice-presidents officials in "elective" office in the normal meaning of the term; they merely form an incidental part of the presidential package.) Cabinet experience cannot properly equip a man who is without an impressive political record.

In the early days of our history the Cabinet was a common way station on the road to the Presidency. Jefferson, Madison, Monroe, John Quincy Adams, and Van Buren—all lifelong politicians—had such service. Recently, only Taft and Hoover—both without elective experience—have had preparation as heads of departments. The two Roosevelts had elective experience, including service as governors of the most populous and cosmopolitan state, and both were assistant secretaries in Washington.

Attitude changes that would support a better use of high appointive posts are clearly suggested by the record and by the study of qualification needs. This may be generalized into a statement of need for greater popular respect for politics, politicians, parties, and the two-party system, including "eggheads" really qualified politically and with public executive experience.

Some of these attitude changes, including some that would improve party functioning, could be effective only when extensive enough to secure changes in statutes or state constitutions. Putting an end to the cross-filing of candidates, cross-voting in primaries, and restrictions on the eligibility of governors for continuing re-election, along with inequitable representational patterns, would provide improvements that require more than popular acquiescence. They depend upon popular insistence. Invention of suitable devices is also required if more candidates are to be made eligible by easing the financial cost and insecurity entailed by political careers.

These things are of the first importance to citizens, both as sovereigns and as subjects. As Professor Stephen K. Bailey of Syracuse University has said, the party system is more essential to freedom than the verbal provisions of the Constitution. And for citizens to be able to delegate their sovereign responsibilities satisfactorily there must be available a fairly large number of well-equipped possibilities. We turn logically, therefore, from political leadership in general to party leadership in particular.

VIII

The Ins and Outs of Politics: Parties

THE MOST important function of citizens is to choose between the alternatives most clearly available to them, most certain to affect policy *generally,* and most capable of clearly identifying responsibility for what is done. These alternatives are not numerous, and they are most manageable for citizens when they are only two. This condition obtains under a two-party system.

The basic choice is always between the "ins" and the "outs," but just what the consequences will be can be appraised with much confidence only when the slants of the "ins" and the slants of the "outs" can be anticipated. This is not possible for citizens when the results will be a coalition government to be negotiated after the election. The real issue is misunderstood when the choice is thought to be principally between two personalities. An intelligent decision is possible and meaningfully clear only when it is to be made between two identifiable parties.

It is useful for voters to ask themselves, when tempted to succumb to personal charm, "Whom would this man appoint to office in his administration?" because the primary power, with most pervasive consequences, which the winner in an election obtains is the power to appoint his principal aides. The average

97

voter would have little ability to guess the actual individuals who would be appointed, of course, and an increase in speculative newspaper stories dealing with this point would confuse rather than clarify the matter. The important and simple fact is that, except for a few situations not important to the present discussion, it is certain that a Republican winner will appoint chiefly Republicans, and a Democratic winner will appoint chiefly Democrats.

The ability of the citizens to put the "ins" out and the "outs" in is crucial to democracy. It results in innumerable small policy shifts because it means putting out a whole incumbent administration and putting in a whole new administration. Its broad consequence is a sustained and varied deference by government to its citizens. Yet the meaning and effectiveness of this ability to expel and to install hinge on the structuring and use of party systems.

The trend to the short ballot, whereby citizens vote for only a few public officials, has been marked for at least three decades. Still, study after study has shown conclusively that very few citizens even recognize the relatively few names they see on ballots. It would be fatuous to imagine that citizens who do not know the names of many principal office-holders and their opponents can judge competently their abilities on an individual basis. Further, when the "ins" who control the legislative branch are of one party and the "ins" who control the executive branch are of another party, it is silly to believe that the citizens at large can have any intelligent notion about who is responsible for what.

Popular failure to identify and use well the principal tools available to popular sovereigns turns largely on a misunderstanding of the importance of parties.

Parties have long been necessary, and are increasingly so because of the growing complexity of society and the multiplicity of public concerns. What many citizens seem impelled to attempt to resolve in terms of relative personal attractiveness of particular candidates involves vastly more. The choice made affects importantly three or more formally differentiated levels of government, at least four levels—adding the international to those of nation, state, and community—of policy, and many categories of policy problems at each level.

Party importance inheres in perhaps six principal functions:

1. Party is the only mechanism yet invented that can make majority government a possible and normal condition, and is therefore the primary known means for insuring the durability of democracy.

2. Parties, much more effectively than individuals, may identify and fix responsibility in terms recognizable by citizens and amenable to voter action. They thus provide for accountability of the in-group and provide ready at hand an alternative out-group.

3. Parties nominate candidates who, if elected, can be held responsible and made accountable through party, even though unknown by name to voters.

4. Parties conduct election campaigns, get-out-the-vote and registration drives, including party membership enrollment.

5. Parties exert an influence which tends somewhat, at least, to unify the parts of the party having different functions—legislative and executive, local, state, and national. So doing, the party provides special lines of communication between officeholders and public, between political leaders in various communities, between jurisdictions and functions, and over the nation at large. This importantly offsets other social factors which contribute to inclinations toward national disintegration.

6. Parties, in competing for majority followership, select moderately different forms of appeal, assume somewhat different positions, and express somewhat divergent characteristics and inclinations. These reflect policy differences which are not sharply delineated, unvarying, or susceptible to use as a basis for *precise* predictions of courses of action in office. Action will be taken later, when conditions have changed somewhat, and under the discipline of responsibility actually assumed. The prior party history, its before-election posture, and its continuing inclination are nevertheless popularly recognizable, important, and roughly valid.

Two Are Company, Three or More a Crowd

A new nation may be for some years a truly democratic one even when a dominant party has no important competitor and when it is much stronger than all opposition groups combined.

This can be true only when strong leadership establishes and maintains democratic method and spirit. This has been the case for more than a decade in India. There, the overwhelmingly dominant Congress party has been thoroughly committed to democratic objectives and procedures; consequently, minority parties have been given exaggerated parliamentary attention. But in the long run a one-party situation is the characteristic device of authoritarian rule.

A third party which is not successful in attracting large followership may provide, in a two-party setting, an element of political dynamism. This is the case when it effectively dramatizes issues of vital character and when its appeal is not merely eccentric or built upon the frustrated ambitions of some individual or group. In other words, a third party may, but rarely does, explore and exploit issue-possibilities too novel for majority acceptance at the moment, thus providing political stimulation. However, if the third party gains much followership it is likely to throw elections to the party least sympathetic to its purpose, and thus to postpone the kind of advancement with which it presumably is concerned.

Once in a century, perhaps, and in some circumstances with slightly greater frequency, it may be also that a third party may emerge to major-party status as an old party disintegrates. As a general rule, however, these two different types of success—dynamic influence politically, or promotion to major-party status by default—are much more hoped for by third-party leaders and followers than either is actually achieved. In most instances, indeed, the third-party movement involves much wastage of political energies. Some such loss of political risk capital is probably desirable in a vital society, but the venturing is usually joined in by the relatively idealistic and unworldly, whose losses often become profits for their political adversaries.

Nations in which multiple-party situations exist are vulnerable to usurpers ruthlessly heading militant minorities. They provide raggedly responsive instruments of government, impair accountability, and transfer to behind-the-scenes negotiations of secondary leaders such primary determinations as are in fact made.

The outcome of a popular election in a multiple-party country cannot be known as a rule when the votes are tabulated. The actual outcome awaits the trades that are later made. A government so established is tentative and inadequate in most cases and in the long run. While some examples of effective multiple-party nations may be cited at any particular time, they are competent despite the party structure and because of other elements of strength existing in their societies. Sometimes the attainment of strength is the result of crisis or external dangers.

Governments differ in manifold subtle ways, and sometimes dramatically. General features of societies must be taken into account if one would understand these governmental differences. Because of social factors not primarily political, the symbolic monarch and the hereditary upper legislative house—both undemocratic in origin—latterly have served democratic ends in a number of instances. Essentially identical laws, so far as verbiage goes, have widely different meanings in application in different countries or jurisdictions. And in some small and homogeneous countries sentimentally unified by sense of kinship, royal symbols, and external dangers, enlightened and effective government has been conducted for several decades through multipartisan politics. The Scandinavian countries are examples. Switzerland is a special case, without close ethnic kinship, with three principal languages, and no unifying royalty; its peculiar economy and its military position set it apart. But these small nations offer no general guidance.

Democratic content of government in practice and the nature of political problems vary from time to time and from country to country in ways we often overlook. An occasional student of government has been inclined to conclude that democracy is possible only in a society whose economy is expanding so rapidly as to make a widening spread of well-being vividly feasible. I am disposed to believe that systematic democracy is most imperative as well as most effective in an expanding economy where the society is large and highly diversified in interest. The English, Scottish, Welsh, and Irish conglomerate seems to me to have an important bearing on the impressive British history. A small and homogeneous society with a stable economy will tend to find internal equilibrium, effecting adjustments through the exercise of more or less informal and sometimes almost unnoticed power forces. In such a society, impersonality is rare, and quiet dominance is likely to accrue to some small minority.

At all events, for the large, far-flung, complex, and advancing society the structure and uses of party have important consequences in terms of the quality and extent of democracy achieved. Within such a society, too, the quality of democracy attained in subordinate jurisdictions is influenced in the same way by the same factors.

One-party municipalities, counties, or states may be said to be less democratic than two-party jurisdictions of the same governmental categories. Such one-party subordinate entities may also be said to be less democratic than the encompassing nation when two conditions obtain. One condition is that a substantial proportion of the subordinate jurisdictions have a two-party character. The second essential is that subordinate one-party jurisdictions so balance or cancel each other that a two-party system can be clearly seen to operate nationally.

The government of a municipality, county, or state may have high acceptability without a corresponding democratic character. What is customary in the immediate environment tends to be less critically considered than the novel and more general. Where livelihood and neighborhood relationships are involved, the inclination is to avoid argument and to be rather unconscious of where power lodges and how it is exercised. Members of the Vermont legislature are rarely importuned by their constituents, while legislators in the bordering but much more cosmopolitan state of Massachusetts feel under many and conflicting pressures.

These phenomena explain or reflect a popular tendency to transfer controversy to higher governmental jurisdictions or to inflate national issues and to deflate local problems. There is a related tendency for citizens to attribute chiefly to national government the political imperfections they have experienced or observed locally.

Because citizens usually seek to avoid local controversies they have some inclination either to adhere to a single party or to renounce partisanship altogether in the community. This is especially true where high homogeneity inclines citizens to hold similar opinions. The result is to leave citizens deprived of the principal instrumentality capable of elevating the general interest over particular interests. The party under strong competition is the primary generalizing vehicle. A simple illustration of the result of local political lethargy is provided by the conservative and competent studies of the Tax Foundation. They show that taxes are levied least in accord with capacity to pay at the local level, and most according to capacity to pay at the national level. A related point is that voters go to the polls in largest numbers for national elections.

Altogether, it seems probable that political vitality, clear responsibility, and pursuit of the general interest are ends best served by a party system so comprehensive that the party attachments of citizens will usually be the same for all levels of government. Partisanship provides a charter for dealing with needed policy differences more likely to be useful locally when it is an aspect of the same mechanism nationally functioning. At the same time, a comprehensive party system will develop more potential political leaders and will provide an escalator for their advancement.

A refinement important to a sound party system is provision for prompt and fair changes in representational patterns to fit population changes. The representational ideal is itself cosmopolitanism, on a per capita basis. Bad representational structures give special influence to some citizens or to some interests. Sometimes these consist of provisions for direct representation of linguistic, religious, or economic groups. Proportional representation, the "corporative state" type of political accreditation for economic interests and other such specializations of the general political mechanism are inimical to democracy, elevating the special and provincial at the expense of the general interest.

In contrast to these mistaken efforts, attention should be given to the ingenious structural proposal for subordinate parts of an enlarged and unified London recently made to a royal commission. This proposal was to shape subordinate entities like wedges of a pie. Each jurisdiction, with very limited functions and these all subject to control by the whole city and by Parliament, would include some citizens living in midtown, some uptown, and still others living in suburbs. Such a structure is in harmony with the general idea that official decision-makers are most likely to make socially sensible decisions if jurisdictions and parties are cosmopolitan in composition.

Applying this thought to parties, as the proposal made to the royal commission would have applied it to jurisdictional form, would require any Labor party to be much broader in membership than its name would imply. An Agrarian party, a Business party, a Senior Citizens party, a Youth party, a Southern party, a Northern party—all of these would be either poorly conceived or poorly named if intended as possible winners of majority followings. For our kind of society, the ideal party system is one in which there are two major parties of about equal strength nationally and in most of the subordinate jurisdictions. Either of the two would be clearly a possible victor in any election almost anywhere throughout the nation.

In practice, a clear-cut and rather certain two-party system has developed in very few nations, and then apparently by happenstance. Majority government apart from a two-party system has been consciously achieved during a crucial period in the modern Federal Republic in Germany by Article 67 of its Constitution. This article, in effect, requires the negative "no confidence" vote conventional in parliamentary governments to be transformed into a positive vote for a new government. This provision enabled the Adenauer government to have a security of tenure that made great achievements possible for it. In the long run the arrangement may also support the emergence of a two-party system.

It is easy for many groups holding different and highly inconsistent views to agree in opposing an "in" government. It is not nearly so easy to find positive agreement on new leadership. The two-party system has demonstrated superior dependability in meeting this fundamental problem of succession. The system may be consciously induced by an arrangement for "runoff" elections in primaries and general elections alike when no candidate has won a majority vote for a particular office, or when no party has won an approximate general majority. Eliminating parties or candidates with small votes can be carried to the point where choice is so limited that parties and candidates do obtain at least an approximate majority. This is a direct route to majority government, an end worth all the time and effort involved.

Majority Government

Qualms about majority government are principally echoes of fears developed long before there was any substantial experience with modern democracies. Those qualms were reflected in the phrase, "tyranny of the majority," suggesting that one way of thinking about everything might be imposed upon everyone. In a society with basic safeguards of freedom, experience has shown that majorities can be constituted only by appealing to many points of view. This is most certainly true in highly cosmopolitan nations. With a wide franchise, a secret ballot, and a two-party system, many minorities associate themselves in mutual defense, and by so doing constitute a majority.

Majority government in a country with our kind of institutions has demonstrated enormous—and significantly growing—deference to minorities. The pattern of civil liberties necessary for this was given to us by great leaders at the time of our national beginning; its adoption did not reflect a conscious and widespread drive by the common people of that time whose descendants have become steadily less tolerant. Rather the opposite is true; because our forefathers built as they did, more and more of us as common folk comprising the citizenry of this country have come to see more clearly the values thus pursued, and to defend them more staunchly.

It is the sectional demagogue—not the democrat, not the nationally elected politician—who attacks and hurts minorities. It is still doubtful whether a direct national referendum on civil liberties would win majority support. Yet national political success can be won only by appealing to the many minorities which would not be so numerous or so important if it were not for the protections provided by Constitution and statutes. This is a "liberal" consequence of the fact that majority government—requiring acceptance by so many citizens—makes for the dominance of moderate views. Fanatics and eccentrics may exist in considerable number, but they are not the stuff of which a majority is made in a highly cosmopolitan nation under structures and procedures designed to serve the values of democracy.

The conclusive case for majority government, once one is committed to democracy, is found by examining the alternatives. Any enduring alternative to majority government is, of course, some kind of minority government. In the long run, benevolence not formally accountable is so unreliable that it must be admitted that minority government inevitably has tyrannous inclinations. Democrats can have no affinity for minority government, and in the present essay we are not committed to an examination of the claims of those who believe in rule by aristocracies. Rather, we are concerned about enhancing democratic effectiveness, and with preventing deterioration.

Majority government is damaged by an undermining of the two-party system. Swelling the membership of a party already dominant in a particular jurisdiction is a blow against democracy. Efforts to make elections nonpartisan—as in choosing mayors, city councils, boards of supervisors, and the like—are further blows. Sneers at partisanship in campaigns designed to make it appear that all really intelligent folk are "independents," are anti-democratic in effect if not in intent. Proportional representation arrangements of all kinds, although advocated in the name of democracy, are in fact hostile to democracy. They make majorities either unattainable or weaker than they should be when the "proportional" spread is to minor parties. They distort and oversimplify the interests of citizens when the proportional distribution of representatives is among economic and functional entities rather than confined to political parties sensitive to and representative of manifold and subtle concerns and values characteristic of an advanced civilization. Representation based directly on economic interest is actually fascistic or syndicalist rather than democratic, and is reminiscent of Mussolini's efforts toward the establishment of a corporative state.

The responsibility of government is for general welfare, general satisfaction. A party vested with responsibility by a majority of citizens can be held accountable for anything and everything of serious popular concern. Individuals chosen to take care of special concerns can at best be held accountable for those. Necessity for action does not stop there, however, and the fundamental task of accommodating all interests in terms of each other remains. This task is of overriding importance, yet no one can be held accountable for it if representatives have been chosen in terms of a lesser, more specialized function.

For effectiveness, democracy in most countries committed to it needs majority rule strengthened. Certainly this is true in the United States. Aside from changes in attitudes and practices of citizens with reference to parties, a few constitutional and statutory changes might wisely be encouraged, and a few others strenuously opposed:

1. Reduce the scope of popular referenda in states where ballots are now loaded with such items; force legislatures to live up to their responsibilities; to do this, deprive them of devices for "passing the buck" to constituents, and otherwise shorten and simplify state constitutions.

2. Leave or create room for citizens readily to initiate action forcing non-gerrymandered redistricting for state, local, and national purposes by a competent *bipartisan* commission assigned to the protection of per capita influence.

3. Make provision for runoff elections whenever either the high candidate or the high party has failed to secure some such proportion as 47 per cent of the total vote cast, the same requirement to apply to primary elections whenever and wherever primaries are held.

4. Avoid completely any effort to require presidential primaries in any more than a small number of states, so that the parties may continue to be charged with the job of making national nominations. Presidential primaries with much binding effect in any very large number of states could ruin parties and frustrate the nominating procedures, besides confining most honorable candidacies to the extremely wealthy.

5. The slow shift to city-wide and county-wide election of such local officials as are popularly chosen should be speeded up and adapted to more situations. Letting county supervisors or aldermen represent and administer districts individually is a practice enhancing parochialism and hostile to good government in the general interest. There should be fewer councilmen and super-

visors, and they should be expected to give general direction to competent executive staffs. Present practice of a different sort invites favoritism and makes political leadership too exclusively personal, too little a matter of party responsibility.

In the same general vein, Chester Barnard proposed some years ago in the *Political Science Review* that the parochialism normally characteristic of the national Congress be reduced and majority government be strengthened by electing in the same package with the president and vice-president a small number of senators and congressmen at large. This would stimulate a good many legislators to demonstrate more concern for the national interest as a way to achieving national political status not now open to them. This device would also make a narrow majority margin wider, the whole administration more unified and effective. The same kind of thing can be helpfully done at the state level of government, too.

6. In somewhat reverse fashion, provision might be made to strengthen minority representation whenever legislative majorities should reach such overwhelming dimensions as, say, 75 per cent. Except in consistently one-party states and subordinate jurisdictions, the purpose in this would be less to strengthen minorities than to overcome parochialism and to develop more broad-gauge party leadership. In either case, the additional representation should not constitute more than 3 or 4 per cent of the membership of any legislative house, and nominations to such at-large posts should be made by party conventions representative of the highest level of government concerned.

7. The residence periods required for voting eligibility in precincts, counties, and states should be sharply reduced. In our highly mobile society, cliques of old residents tend to dominate state and local party organizations in a most undemocratic fashion. Shortening residence requirements is an essential, but insufficient, reform. New residents will also need to pursue vigorous courses of political action to secure equitable shares of influence.

How Different Should Parties Be?

A nation in which there were two major parties "as like as two peas" would not be wholly ill served by them if each was not merely a possible beneficiary of impromptu and random support but possessed of a firm following large enough to be thought capable of winning any election. The Tweedledee party, out of office, would be a constant threat to the incumbent Tweedledum party. Thus there would be always available to voters an alternative to the government in power, capable of being vested with power at will and in an orderly fashion. This would provide the primary essentials of popular government.

Because of the presence of the alternative, the "ins" would be trying to extend their following, the "outs" would be trying to identify new or different and more appealing ways to win support. Even from the beginning, the Tweedledees would think of themselves as "us" and of the Tweedledums as "them," thus exaggerating differences between them. The Tweedledums would be going through the same process of differentiating themselves from the "out" party. Each party would inevitably have a history somewhat different from that of the other, which would result in being defensive of different actions and in having somewhat different sources of membership and different reasons for affiliations.

The Tweedledee and Tweedledum parties thus, in fact, would not be "as like as two peas," but would be recognizably different in ways on the whole rather hard to verbalize. In a familiar form, a sense of the differences is expressed by the banker's wife who refuses to call on a new neighbor because she hears that the neighbor is a Democrat, the union leader's wife who objects to the inclusion of a Republican woman in a neighborhood bridge club, a union member's wife who votes Republican to better her social relationships as her economic status improves, and by many others in similar ways. Deeply felt emotions turn on party differences that some citizens assert are unreal or not great enough to be significant.

Actually, differences between the two major parties in this country are about as great as they are in any country where political order obtains, and about as great, year in and year out, as social and political health requires or permits. The differences are substantial enough so that the voters may, in successive elections, carry the country to any extremes that may be thought desirable, but small enough so that we do not really go to any very extreme point without trial and deliberation. The differences are small enough so that we are not forced continually to back up a step every time we take two steps forward, and we certainly avoid a course whereby any election may effect a revolution which could cause the next election to be a counterrevolution.

The impatient and the unworldly may want much more than this. A good many persons with very strong opinions may in all sincerity and public spirit be most unhappy because the majority does not force the government to a course of action that they are sure is the most desirable one. We are politically organized to enable the majority to control, and to prevent any individual or any minority, however sincere, from writing the ticket for us all. And what a majority will accept in a condition of political order is bound to be usually not more than mildly different from what the majority is used to and has found acceptable.

An erroneous notion widely held in this country is that a proper two-party system is one in which one party is militantly "liberal" and another party as emphatically "conservative." This notion probably derives in part at least from vague familiarity with the names of European parties. A greater familiarity would reveal the lack of meaning in these names. In any case, reflection will carry the conviction that a militantly "liberal" party would win an election only in time of desperate crisis; that if the nation should survive a crash program produced by the inexperienced vested with power because of popular desperation, much of what was done in that emergency régime would be undone by its successor. Advancement is not often to be secured because an action is "liberal" or "conservative," but because it is needed, feasible, and acceptable.

What is acceptable to a majority is most unlikely to resemble some aggressive individual's idea. Individuals as a whole prefer old ways, the familiar, the orderly, the habitual. Political leaders are those who can find ways to please the majority in doing the necessary. Party is hence the principal means by which majority acceptance is explored and authenticated. A party that has a chance of winning in any circumstances short of acute crisis, when our very national survival is in grave question, will be an essentially moderate party. We have had a few administrations nationally, and a larger number in subordinate jurisdictions, characterized by timidity, but every effective national administration in our history has been led and dominated by *strong* moderates.

What was done was in line with our past history and our developing character, our outreachings, our needs. Little was undone afterwards, yet every major, controversial action of our most active administrations could have been reversed later except the declarations of war. In those cases of war wherein we had first been attacked, we had no choice, and support was nearly unanimous. In the other cases, for all the tragedy involved, the majority support was real and heavy.

The party difference, then, aside from splinter parties, is only in part and on occasion significantly ideological; even then it is not a sharp, uniformly spread, or monumental difference. Voters differ widely in inclination to think in abstract terms, and on the occasions when there are objects to which they will express commitment in general terms. At one stage in the period of Franklin D. Roosevelt it seemed that the people were voting primarily for a new "in" party; at another stage they were chiefly supporting a movement—an attack on the depression and on unemployment; at still another stage they seemed more definitely to be following a man and a party in whose determination to act helpfully they had come to believe strongly. All of these elements were probably present in varying amounts throughout the three stages. In the end—but only then—it became clear that almost every one of the surviving new programs would get favorable votes from a large majority of the citizens. The opposition party never saw political gain in trying to liquidate the principal programs, which endured through years of their own leadership.

However accurate these views may be, the fact remains that only the testing methods of politics reveal authoritatively what will appeal—and when—in general terms, what in particular terms, and whether the general "principle" or the specific action will be approved. But experienced politicians can make some educated guesses. They would generally assert, for example, that while nearly everybody emphatically believes abstractly in budget-balancing, few would readily vote particular tax increases to achieve it, or vote repeal of particular expenditures that would provide it in the only other possible way.

People who work at politics develop a keen sensitivity to such inclinations, and apart from formal government itself, political parties are the only means for identifying and testing them widely. Parties are ways of formulating and identifying alternatives which may be acceptable to a majority, ways for assigning authority, and ways of holding accountable those who exercise authority in our name. *The little difference we can see at any one election time is highly important; it is worth all the fervor with which we approach it.* Over a period of time these little differences can add to monumental totals, each winning party dragging the other a little way in its direction, for a while, at least. We should be glad that we do not in any single election cast our ballots for centuries ahead. Nor should we be surprised to find that the long future is not what the one election is all about.

Voters with Frayed Party Ties

Voters wholly without party affiliations are usually referred to as "independents," though there are varying degrees of independence and different ways to exercise it. The complete independent is sometimes disposed not to play any organizational role, consciously or unconsciously inclined to a kind of political and social celibacy. Other independent voters may submit rather readily to organizational disciplines other than those of politics. Some are notably patriotic and idealistic, even though given to great exaggeration of the general acceptability of their own political judgments.

The existence of a minority of rather completely independent citizens is probably both inevitable and necessary to the working of democracy. An independent minority makes a direct political contribution peculiar to its free-wheeling character. It contributes also to the exercise of more limited and often better directed and more effective independence of party members. It is one part of the general phenomenon of uncertainty about the outcome of elections which is thoroughly desirable.

In some measure it is undoubtedly true that reason contributes to the political activity of independents. It is obvious, too, that

rational considerations should weigh in the political scales, even
if not preponderantly, and certainly not to the point of excluding
all other factors. (As Woodrow Wilson, the only professional intellectual ever to come to the Presidency, remarked: "Man is
much more than a 'rational being,' and lives more by sympathies
and impressions than by conclusions. . . . Persuasion is a force,
but not information.") It is also obvious that democracy would
have little meaning if party allegiance were complete and permanent. But it is not so obvious that not all independence is
good, that voting "for the best man" is not a sufficient guide, that
independents may be too numerous, or too readily mobile, and
may damage parties to the detriment of all of us.

The role of complete independents is more limited than most
of them realize. They deprive themselves of any part in the
nominating process. They deprive themselves of the strength
which comes from formal and directed association with others;
for once they become members of a political-action group, even
though not a party, they abandon complete independence. A
fusion-ticket organization, of course, is a third political party.
The maximum augmentation of an independent's strength is
achieved when, after he makes up his mind what top candidate
to vote for, he votes a straight—or very nearly straight—ticket of
the party whose top nominee he has chosen. If he is unwilling to
do this he had better look again at the top candidate he has
chosen. In other words, he is most effective when, for the moment,
his major choice is a particular party. One exception to this dictum is that for offices in subordinate jurisdictions that are strongly and rather permanently held by a single party, he might wisely
vote for the second party's candidates. Every vote that supports
the attainment of a two-party situation enhances the influence of
independents and supports the realization of actual democracy.

The ticket-scratcher may be something other than a complete
independent. A party member who understands his role will find
that two great resources as a voter are his ability to help create a
two-party condition and, in jurisdictions where that condition
already obtains, to give preference to the definitely abler and
more honorable candidate occasionally found on the ticket of the
opposition party, as a way of pressing his own party to seek more

nominees of similar caliber. He is warranted in doing this, as a loyal partisan, when the difference between the two candidates is clear and substantial, when the voter himself has been really active in supporting abler nominees than those his party has chosen, and when scratching is reluctantly practiced.

The various shades and manners of party independence can be well appraised only on a basis of some inventory of the present shortcomings and weaknesses of parties and the failures of well disposed citizens to make sufficiently positive contributions to them. Too many intelligent citizens with good intentions do not know how unacquainted they are with parties, party functions, and party needs. Too many confuse party organization with an undesirable "bossism." Too many expect to be granted party eminence for irrelevant reasons, without having first earned it by long, hard work under the discipline of party leaders. The most important betterment of government in America is to be made at the level of parties by unself-seeking people who will so learn and earn as to be able to help achieve it.

A handicap to the effectiveness of some citizens is their curious notion that, however useful parties may be at the national and state levels, partisanship is wholly out of place at the local level. Yet majority government is unrecognizable if ever present at all without a party system. Accountability is clouded without it. The political nature of democracy is denied without it. The party system would not exist nationally—or certainly would exist only tenuously— if it did not exist at the local level.

There will always be a great deal of disagreement within any party capable of getting majority support. The net difference between the two parties is on the whole more definite, however, and more uniformly widespread, than many voters seem to realize. Locally as well as nationally in this country one party tends to be closer to the "common people" than does the other. Locally as much as nationally one party tends to try to meet mass needs directly, while the other party tries to achieve equally satisfactory results by indirect methods—primarily relying upon private business and private benevolence.

This is a legitimate line of general differentiation. It distinguishes different approaches, sometimes not very distinct, to the provision of care for the needy, provision for education, methods of dealing with epidemics, provision of sanitary facilities and other health arrangements (general hospitals, mental institutions, restaurant and soda fountain inspection, meat, dairy, and ice cream plant inspection), the handling of union pickets, sit-in-demonstrators, and street orators. All of these matters are illustrative of ancient local governmental responsibilities which today provide the great bulk of local government's work. Yet these activities of local government are merely the local version of the principal domestic issues treated at national and state governmental levels.

Neither party when in power will treat all these matters in the same way in all communities. Yet the general party difference in attitudes and manners affecting these policy fields is sufficiently consistent to argue strongly for more voting consistency and more reliance on party responsibility locally than many voters demonstrate.

Finally, even in a summary treatment of this important matter, the citizen seems to need reminding that the local party is the source of most political leadership at higher levels. The fact that a mayor who makes an especially good record may hope to become lieutenant-governor, governor, or United States senator is the strongest general incentive to good local government.

Poverty-stricken Parties

Parties are first of all local and state entities. At the national level the party is nebulous except in its finest flowering in the national presidential nominating conventions. Aside from this it has some being in the national committee, and some in the loose-jointed party delegations in the two houses of Congress. For the party in power, the president, his department and agency heads, and the high-level office staffs of the executive branch present still another party facet. These are not parts of a strong and clear unity, but different aspects of a complex phenomenon.

The divisions of government—its branches and its jurisdictional levels—cause somewhat similar divisions of party elements. Many members of Congress rely on personal organizations more than on party, while big-city party organizations characteristically have little concern about what the national government does once they have prevented any opposition organization from putting their men into congressional posts. The national party committee is largely dependent upon state and local party organizations for support—particularly for financial support and for essential grass-roots work. In other words, there is little the national party can do for state and local organizations, and the national party, somewhat like the national Congress, is excessively beholden to its "subordinate" parts with more parochial responsibilities.

These things are true in spite of the fact that without formal and distinct party organizations total national disunity would be much greater than it is now. Party organizations do assume and further certain common objectives, do facilitate communication and more or less concerted action. They do provide a way in which numerous citizens may work at and otherwise contribute to public business without actually, in most cases, becoming dependent upon party for income. The real troubles with the party system in America are these: parties are not unified enough in terms of the three levels of government; too few citizens work hard enough for them; too few work at politics with no direct self-interest involvements; and too many attempt to prove their quality as citizens by attacking as "machine politicians" those other citizens who do suffer the heat and burden of the day.

In the absence of workers of a different kind, and lacking dependable and sufficient funds for the hiring of staffs, the party organizations' rank-and-file personnel will continue to be hangers-on, petty job seekers, and persons who have worked out some formula whereby they may make a living and at the same time express some kind of natural inclination toward gregariousness and interest in the political way of life. The formula may be honorable, dubious, or downright dishonest in particular cases and settings. Lawyers comprise the largest, and most readily identifiable, category of citizens who can combine personal career and politics. In many cases they combine the two in ways not yet strictly unlawful but nonetheless tending toward corruption of the governmental processes to the advantage of "clients."

In some states one way of staffing party organizations systematically is worked out by informal agreement between the two parties when certain legislative committee staffs and the staffs of majority and minority leaders are frankly but quietly enlarged so as to serve party, as distinguished from legislative, purposes. This is an enlargement of the practice of appointing party chairmen to Cabinet jobs at both national and state levels, while leaving all or most of their official responsibilities to be carried by deputies.

Practices mentioned in the two preceding paragraphs and the use of other appointive jobs for political "patronage" have been the principal means whereby parties have been kept alive. These are most common and extensive at local and state levels and account in very large part for the general ill repute of politics and parties. By some quirk of popular judgment the opinion derived from familiarity with state and local levels is pointed most viciously against the national parties and the national government, where the practices are less resorted to for the simple reason that they offer little political advantage there.

Patronage is less and less useful in all levels of politics, and there are known ways of using party clearance with no impropriety and no impairment of quality of personnel in a very small proportion of the public jobs where there might thereby be some positive gain in responsibility, quality of performance, and party effectiveness. It is not necessary to go into these things here. What is important here is to emphasize the very narrow range within which patronage nowadays offers any real partisan advantage in ways sometimes attributed to it. Local and state party organizations have not discovered new and better ways of maintaining themselves. They are much too limited to familiar practices.

It is also important to emphasize here the basic poverty of parties in terms of competent staff resources for research, campaign, and office purposes; in terms of between-campaigns party workers, campaign workers, and money.

Money is not the whole of this, of course. Nor should all of the money going to parties be private money, for private gifts tend to be associated with private obligations. Basic financial provisions for the parties at every level of government should be made by the national government, because this would support party coherence at successive levels, and because the provision would most certainly be done equitably and honorably there. States might make additional allowances. Private contributions to parties thus would become incidental, and party financial concerns would be separated and freed from the obligations that unavoidably are associated with campaign aid to individuals prior to nomination. In any case, to supply parties with the no-strings-attached resources they need, whether through government or through private gifts or through hard work, is an obligation of citizenship long evaded in stuffy condescension, misunderstanding, or preoccupation with other matters.

IX

Communication by, to, and among Citizens

As BREATH, food, and drink are to physical being, so is communication to human society. Yet as one may "dig his own grave with his teeth," so may one talk himself and his associates or his government into dislike, misunderstanding, confusion, and grossly wasted time.

Studies of morale in business organizations have shown no significant relationship between employees' attitudes toward their companies and the amount of information they have about the companies. Rather, in work relationships the communication that gets results is of specific kinds—providing direction, guidance, and instruction in terms of quite concrete job needs.

The typical organizational employee wants to go on being employed, wants to be reasonably assured and confident in his job. If he has been informed and directed so that he knows how to do his job satisfactorily with a minimum of surplus talk and supervision, his job-communication needs will have been pretty well met.

It is probable that this is more true about the job of being a citizen-sovereign than we have been inclined to believe. We have tended to feel that we should be more thoroughly knowledgeable about the whole business of government than we really can be.

Even an occasional, ill-equipped Cabinet member new to his job has been known to act as if he thought he should know everything being done in his department. This is both impossible and undesirable. The department head needs to be intelligently selective about the information he develops, and he needs most of all to know *how* things are done in his department so that he may change those things he finds needing to be changed. The citizen, operating at a still higher level of responsibility, requires information appropriate to a still more general kind of judgment.

As citizens we have been poorly instructed, poorly informed. We have been prone to have "judgments" about specifics we fail to understand. Information and pseudo information available to us is more likely to disturb, to confuse, or merely to interest us trivially, than to illumine our sovereign position. The press is too full of pretentious trivia and too much comment is scheduled by the hour, day, or week, and not according to the stock of useful comment. Altogether there is a tendency to equate the quantity of verbiage with the quality of democracy.

For us as citizens it is even truer than for a department head that it is both impossible and undesirable to know about everything being done in all the agencies of all the levels of government. Our time and minds are too limited, our concerns of other kinds too numerous for any such objective to be sensible. The communication processes useful to our responsibilities are not the same as those useful within the formal structures of operating government. We need to know about intragovernmental communication methods only as such knowledge facilitates our efforts as citizens to communicate and to receive communications.

It should be useful to know, for example, that in the national government those agencies of government that have many dealings with many citizens are extremely receptive and attentive to what the citizens say about them and their programs. Nationwide programs are not remote from the people, even if their headquarters are in the District of Columbia.

Citizen to Government

In my experience in Washington I found that the many individuals and groups from various parts of the country who called in my office to complain about program activities never told me anything I had not already been told by department personnel. This does not mean that the travelers wasted their efforts, because the foreknowledge that they were going to come to Washington may have inspired the reports. A trip to the national capital is indicative of an intensity of citizen feeling which is almost certain to be the subject of prior administrative report in any agency widely exposed.

Visitors from the field who had first visited subordinate offices and then had come to mine, however, on occasion brought me useful information about the way they had been received. Correspondence from the field, and letters and calls from members of Congress, did add most helpfully, too, to the general body of administrative intelligence. Usually reflecting more particular sentiments and less intensity of citizen feeling than personal visits, what these reports brought was news to the office of the Secretary of Agriculture because subordinate personnel had not anticipated its reaching us, had not appraised it as important enough to justify their reporting it, or had not themselves been informed about it. Their own physical energies and working hours, and my own, were too limited to permit communication of all conceivable field reactions. A great deal must be left to these other media when and if citizen concern becomes sufficient to feel need of expression. But these and other devices do in combination give top administrators of widely exposed agencies a very adequate knowledge of how citizens throughout the country feel about what their agencies are doing.

For the instances of intense feeling, even about matters of much less than earth-shaking import, the bureaucracy tends rather unfailingly to anticipate citizen communication. I recall a bureau chief who called me to say that I could expect telephone calls within a day or two from both senators from a certain rather sparsely populated state. "We are transferring from their principal city a very popular man who, nearing retirement age, is becoming less able to handle the active job he has there," said the bureau chief. "If we leave him there he will get into a situation of serious personal embarrassment, but by transferring him to a less physically exacting job we enable him to go on to retirement happily with no loss in pay, although with loss of future increases he probably has anticipated. He is a good man, has served us well, and has been a great joiner of local organizations, so there will be very sincere objections." I was called by one of the senators within an hour, and by the second one the following morning. I told them exactly what I had been told, and they took no further exception to the transfer.

I could readily cite scores of similar examples because it is an axiom in any sophisticated public agency that one should tell "the boss" in advance about troublesome things he is likely to hear about anyway. He has many ways of hearing, at parties and meetings, on field trips, at congressional hearings, from party workers, or from competitive peers who are eager to pass on gossip they have heard which has critical implications.

It is somewhat similarly axiomatic that information must be passed higher up the hierarchy if it is likely to be of interest there, whether implying criticism or not. Staff assistants become very sensitive to what their chief will attend to, and are anxious not to be found guilty of failing to pass on types of intelligence valued by him. One example of the way this process works will suffice.

A New York industrialist was one of two men who raised money to buy the two Roosevelt houses near Hunter College to give to the college for special use and preservation. They had an appropriate portrait of the President for the house in which he had lived, but were not certain which portrait of the President's mother to procure for her house next door. The industrialist instructed the vice-president of his company to "go down to Washington and ask the President to decide."

The executive came to Washington and telephoned successively each of the persons whose names he had heard as having White House positions. He somehow was unable to reach any of them. He thereupon asked me to call and make the appointment for him. I refused to do this, on the ground that I sought appointments for persons only when their business with the President was in the area of my personal responsibility. But I assured him that he could easily get the appointment he sought if he would simply tell his story to the operator on the White House switchboard who was first on the line there. He did this, and had an interesting half-hour with the President.

The behind-the-scenes story as I imagined it in advance must have unfolded in fact about this way: The switchboard operator hearing the story thought to herself, "I'd better tell the chief operator about this." The chief operator in turn thought, "I'd better tell General Watson's secretary." (General Watson was the appointments secretary.) The General's secretary in turn thought to herself, "I'd better tell the General about this." And when the General heard about it he thought to himself, "The boss will probably want to see this fellow; I'd better ask him."

The story illustrates a very large part of the citizen-to-government communication process. It suggests the error in thinking that one must go directly to the top, and hints the subtler fact that it is less necessary to reach the top even indirectly than most people would believe. Sophisticated organizational people, in dealing with organizations other than their own, by preference work with subordinates most of the time. Only one of a number of reasons for this is that if subordinates are hostile to a particular line of action they can find innumerable technical reasons by which they convince their superiors that it should not be pursued. A corollary thought is that the citizen who attempts to use "influence" will inspire special opposition by subordinates; the latter will feel that if the effort were not to get them to do something improper which would later redound to their own discredit, the use of influence would not be attempted.

Subordinates will also resent inroads on their own responsibilities. I recall many examples, in and out of government, and refer here to one in the organization of a national magazine. The president of the magazine company happened to come to my office just after having hired as "Washington editor" a man of considerable reputation. He mentioned this to me with satisfaction. I asked him what his editor-in-chief thought of the selection, and he replied, "I'm sure he'll be pleased. I'll tell him about it when I get back to New York." His appointee lasted exactly one year.

Concerned citizens stand a better chance of securing satisfaction when they use top officials as impersonal channels to an operating organization, and hold top officials responsible after the fact, rather than try to get top officials to decide individually and initially. It should be said, too, that even if a citizen feels that he must personally call upon a high official he should have his business stated in writing to leave behind him. Otherwise he would be assuming that the busy official would have both the time and the inclination to formulate it himself for transmission to and consideration by his organization. Furthermore, there must be records of government business so that it may be fully reviewed later, and the citizen should prefer his own statement of what he proposed to one prepared by someone else.

Letters not personally presented but sent through the mails are given careful attention in every real two-party jurisdiction, and generally in national agencies conducting widespread programs. Letters may be written to numerous recipients and with persistence. Up to a point, persistence is impressive and gets additional attention. Beyond that point (which may be described in over-systematic but illustrative terms as the top center spot in a bell-shaped curve) attention diminishes somewhat, as earlier it had increased.

Intensity of feeling is believed to attach to persistence in writing, and the more intensely a citizen feels, the more is the desire to mollify him. Replies to his successive letters, therefore, usually will be signed by progressively higher officials after progressively higher level examination of the matter in question. But when at high levels there is a conviction that every possible consideration has been given to the persistent letter writer, successive replies to his epistles will be shorter and signed at successively lower hierarchal levels. The perceptive citizen can interpret his government mail accordingly.

Most of the interchange involved in the preceding discussion will probably—and preferably—relate to the concerns of citizens as subjects rather than as sovereigns. In their sovereign function, citizens should try to influence *public* opinion, and otherwise should communicate policy proposals to legislators, top executive officials, and party leaders.

In this connection it is desirable to emphasize the difference between agencies with farflung domestic exposures and those whose functions are further removed and less often encountered. The State Department, for example, has little occasion for direct dealing with many citizens except in the handling of passports. The Defense Department's citizen dealings are usually very limited in scope because of being confined rather strictly to suppliers. By the same token, when citizens feel disposed to communicate with these agencies they are more likely to be moved by general, patriotic concerns than by self-interest and personal involvement. Direct communication between such citizens in any great numbers and the departments concerned is much less usual and much more difficult than communication between the farmers and the handlers and processors of farm products on the one hand, and the Department of Agriculture on the other. Sometimes, but by no means invariably, a few communications from citizens weigh disproportionately in the scales of policy judgment of those who receive little mail from citizens, just as editorial judgment of a particular columnist or comic strip artist may be influenced by a handful of letters.

Direct communication, then, is by no means out of the question or futile. But the sovereign function is much more appropriately and effectively served, as a rule, by persistent and thoughtful seeking of information and explanations of policy than by raw affirmations of settled opinion. Indeed, it may be that the most important advice about communication that may be given to citizens is to use the method of inquiry and the display of interest, certainly including approbation when that is the attitude. Questions asked, and praise given, actually stimulate official thinking. For this purpose, letters may be addressed to legislators, to party committees, to the chief executive, and to department, agency, or bureau heads. Letters should be succinct, and as often as possible indicated as requiring no reply. The point is that the self-seekers and the snap-judgment chaps are expressing themselves freely; the sovereignty-oriented citizens should do as much. By all means they should encourage honesty, frankness, courage, leadership, and citizen education by officials, in the absence of which demagogy, parochialism, triviality, and personal magnetism will prevail.

As was brought out at a meeting of newspaper editors in August, 1959, the average level of educational attainment in this country has been rising rapidly and significantly in recent decades, but it appears that neither the press, the entertainment industry, nor the advertising agencies will recognize the fact and raise their standards higher except at the demand of citizens. Citizens, in turn, need to develop the kind of perspective that subordinates crude self-interest and strives toward thinking and judging in terms more appropriate to their sovereign responsibilities.

Between Citizens

Without a sustained effort, citizens will communicate generally with citizens who belong to the same club, are in a similar economic or status situation, have roughly the same kind of background and similar goals. Many citizens do not really know anyone who belongs to any political party but their own. They talk glibly about politics and political figures, but in their social isolation have not the vaguest real acquaintance with the world in which political leaders live. There are even occasional United States senators who are elected from very homogeneous states because of engaging personal manners, who could not be elected to even a minor office on a national ticket. In the House there is a somewhat larger number of nonpolitical—but bitterly partisan—members.

This is not intended to suggest that anyone should hypocritically fraternize with those not really congenial. It is intended to suggest that citizen-sovereigns have a duty to diversify associations enough to stimulate thinking about a society which includes members with many different slants and concerns.

Such thinking cannot be done in the absence of some acquaintance with, some understanding of, some real sympathy with, the hopes, needs, and affections of a goodly number of persons quite differently situated from one's self. And this can be useful only when it is, in particular instances, productive of real respect and liking. This communication should be interpersonal, interstate, interparty, across interest lines and status levels.

Intercitizen communication on public affairs can wisely be engaged in more judicially than is now the usual manner. Let us be as much democracy's advocate and exemplar as its critic of poor performance.

Communication by Government

The duty of "the government" in respect to its citizens is to determine policies, to carry on programs in realization of policies, and to explain to and educate the citizens about these policies, programs, and the problems that lie in and behind them.

The explanatory and educational responsibilities have become heavier and more difficult with the advance of civilization. At the same time, there are recognizable tendencies on the part of officials to become more exclusively listeners, less often and less meaningfully teachers and expositors. There are special reasons, in addition to the increase in problem complexity, for these tendencies.

One of the contributing factors is the sustained congressional hostility to anything more than dull and stodgy departmental publications and press releases, and to speeches by civil servant-executives designed to enlarge citizen participation in governmental programs. This hostility is not a new phenomenon; rather, it is the new complexity of problems which requires more skill in explaining programs and makes the explanations both in appearance and in fact evangelical.

Once Congress or the legislature has approved a statute authorizing a program, it becomes the duty of executive officers to make it known, to make its authorized services actually available and useful. Objections to such promotional material by legislators is not according to party lines in many instances, but often reflects a desire to hold down public participation in the program and thereby to hold down expenditures. In other instances objections reflect confused feeling that civil servants should be neutrons, or at least not competitive with legislators in the publicity media. In still other instances the feeling is that the publicity is an effort to bring pressure upon the legislative body. For these and other reasons Congress or particular members use or threaten to use appropriations sanctions to punish aggressive and imaginative promotion of programs.

The fact that there is a Joint Congressional Committee on Printing which controls printing of the executive branch in detail is another expression of a negative attitude toward departmental efforts to reach citizens. And it is true, of course, that program promotion can be converted quickly and subtly into propaganda or agitation for enlarged legislative support.

Legislators themselves are under a somewhat similar discipline. Single strong private interests in a particular constituency need not use overt threats to lead their representatives to a preference for weasel words. In an earlier day only the agrarian interest was similarly powerful in a great majority of the legislative jurisdictions. Further, diminished general respect for political figures— nurtured by strong private interests and accelerated somewhat by naive political scientists of a generation ago—has gone along with a popular misinterpretation of democracy which sees it as an organ of response rather than as one of responsible and accountable leadership.

The most important limitation on political leaders' capacity to educate and inform is a consequence of an equally grievous and even more widespread misinterpretation of democratic order. This is the devaluation of party resulting from a kind of intellectual snobbery pattern established a few decades ago. In consequence, millions of persons today seem to feel that they prove their intelligence and virtue by proclaiming, "I always vote for the *man*."

The results of this proud adherence to irresponsibility are steadily mounting. They tend to push each officeholder into a position where he is a solitary individual, deprived of the strength that inheres in unity with colleagues and party. They tend to create a situation in which nobody is particularly responsible for anything except inoffensive personal appearance and manners. One of the aspects of this tendency is to steer each official in the direction of becoming a yes man to an uninformed public, just as surviving executives in a badly run business become yes men to their superiors.

Agreeing with the strong private interests in one's constituency, and accepting little responsibility for interpreting public problems as they appear in official perspective, the elective official may clothe himself with the appearance of strength by resorting to demagoguery. Only the maverick and the eccentric are sure to get headlines, and party leadership may be mere horse trading rather than policy articulation.

What has just been said relates to tendencies; it does not purport to be a full description of our present condition. It points to what may be the direction of our movement. The point is simply that for a variety of reasons it seems that the role of public education by elective officials is a diminishing one. Yet surely those elected to office should be middlemen between both the citizens and the government, and the government and the citizens. Elected officials should be our principal instructors in public affairs. At the national level—and usually elsewhere—this means the chief executive and the members of the legislative body. The latter, of course, are most numerous and must therefore carry most of the responsibility for instructing the general public.

A certain senator of more than ordinary integrity once explained his vigorous championship of some influential but overweeningly selfish constituents by saying, "They came first to see me; if I don't get behind them, my colleague will." (The colleague was of the same party.) Acting alone, their conduct finds a low common denominator; acting together, they might do less in support of their constituents' pursuit of special favors.

In other cases, a party caucus or even a House resolution might take a high position which no one or two legislators could hold alone, but the caucus would have to possess real cohesion and some disciplinary powers such as election of committee chairmen would tend to provide. Individual legislators then could and should defend and explain problems and policy in a more responsible fashion.

In part, but only in part, the weakness of political parties in this country is the result of citizen attitudes. It is not altogether clear, either, how citizens may undo the damage they have caused, particularly in restoring and elevating the educational function of officials and party leaders. There is so much lack of party unity: each party has a different version of itself in different sections of the country if not quite in every state; each party has one semblance in its formal committees, its executive officials, and its nominating conventions, another semblance in the United States Congress, and sometimes, at least, in the legislatures of particular states.

Relating these things to the function of communication alone, it might be found useful if citizens would do much more letter-writing of the kind that simply seeks policy elucidation, addressing these inquiries more often to party committeemen and party chairmen, and secondarily to the appointive political executives, and perhaps less often to legislators. If the relationship of the inquiring citizen to his party should be extended in still other direction, in all cases as free as possible from narrow self-interest, the result would be to strengthen the party relative to the legislature, without weakening the latter. In time, this might prove highly salutary.

In the first instance and at the national level, at least, many legislators would resent party committee inquiries on behalf of interested citizens. It would be regarded as something new, probably reflecting an officious intention. The congressman and his staff would wonder why the citizen inquiry had not come directly to him. At the same time, the inquiry could hardly be dealt with roughly, and by the time a whole congressional generation has found this a frequent occurrence there might be a greater tendency to share responsibility somewhat and thereby to strengthen parties at a point where they are now crucially weak.

Members of Congress are much more alert in defense of Congress than they are in defense of their party. On the other hand, individual members of Congress are a poor tool for citizens at large, which is the position of citizens consciously trying to live up to their sovereign responsibilities. The Congress as a whole is a good tool for sovereign citizens only about as far as unified parties within it assume responsibility as separate parties. Only the particular party in Congress and the particular national party of which it is an expression can articulate and communicate a policy that serves the needs of sovereign citizens, and one for which accountability is clear.

The policy may on many occasions be a policy of agreeing with the policy of the other party. When there is significant disagreement, however, it should be in more cases clearly a disagreement

between parties. Both agreement and disagreement in these terms
are communicable, understandable, and therefore accountable.
Highly individualized and highly parochial expressions not identified as party positions, on the other hand, usually provide little
communication useful in the formation of popular majority positions on the part of citizens responsibly concerned with their
sovereign duties.

Legislative-Executive Communication

The intent of the preceding paragraphs has been to point up
the importance to citizens of more frequent and clearer functioning of legislative bodies in terms of party coherence and responsibility. This is important to useful communication between legislators and citizens. The intent has not been to attack or to de-
mean the legislative bodies, but to suggest how they may be made
more popularly significant and useful, if perhaps sometimes and
in some ways less interesting, erratic, or imponderable. In one
way, even now, especially at the level of the national Congress, the
legislature plays a role in communication most essential to democratic government. This role is that of constant and resourceful
inquirer into the manners and actions of the executive branch.

The congressional investigating committee has special uses and
special significance. But the function now being acclaimed is the
daily business of finding out what is going on throughout the
government by individual inquiry of representatives, senators,
their staff members, and the members of committee staffs. The
legislative organ of a two-party jurisdiction is more thoroughly
representative of the multiple concerns of citizens than any other
single body. On the average, members are tough, intelligent, and
competent, besides collectively possessing great power over the
repute, activities, and personal fortunes of most persons within
the executive branch. In their respective constituent jurisdictions
these officials see a vast deal of actual governmental operations.
They hear constantly from constituents. Thus equipped, it should
not be surprising that they give the most meticulous attention to
inquiries, entailing the use of many thousands of man-years of
official time, and tens of millions of dollars in expenditures by
the executive branch in investigating, studying, and replying.

The time and money are very substantially less than the value of the activity to the American people and to the cause of democratic government.

The legislative body—especially the national Congress—is thoroughly representative, and it is at the same time responsible as no private entities can be. The Congress shares with the executive and judicial branches responsibility for the government, and members are generally patriotic people. The Congress and the executive officials are also directly accountable to the people, vulnerable before them, and sensitive to tides of sentiment and expressions of concern.

While sharing governmental responsibility with the executive branch, the Congress also is competitive with it in function, and often in interest. The Congress also has a definite two-party character. While all members of Congress are strongly disposed to search for any kind of incompetence or unfairness or malfeasance, those who belong to the party in opposition to the president in office at the particular time are louder, especially tireless, and often ruthless in such searches. Congress as a body, in contrast with private competitors, in its approach to executive performance is representative, responsible, competitive, and critical, even though individual members vary widely in ability.

Literally millions of requests for information are made to the executive branch annually by or on behalf of members of Congress. Most of these are as promptly and as fully answered as the organizational and technical character of the material and the act of responding permit. The presumption is—everywhere outside of the defense-involved area—that *of course* members of Congress are entitled to all information they seek. F.B.I. investigational findings and some other administrative investigational data are subject to some limitations in deference to pledges of protection for those who have given information in confidence. But there are several ways in which congressional needs may be and are met, even in these exceptional cases. High officials in one case may arrange to read to the inquiring member, in a face-to-face session at which notes cannot be taken but the possession of the actual record may be demonstrated, the material in question without revealing or indicating the names of informers. Or in some cases a highly honorable member may be permitted to read a record while a copy of it is refused him.

In any case, inquiries from congressmen and committees not answered freely constitute a small decimal percentage of those made which are not related to defense, and refusal is not decided upon except at a very high executive level. In some cases only a presidential refusal would be ventured; in others it might be made by a Cabinet member but after consultation with the president; in still others the Cabinet member would feel certain enough of general congressional acceptance of his position to make the refusal on his own responsibility. The refusal would almost never be made below the level of a department head's office.

Any refusal of information is subject, of course, to congressional complaint and retribution. It is a fact of the greatest significance that Congress as a body has almost never taken an action that might be construed as punitive for withholding information that should have been given. Individual members, sometimes for home effect, do complain once in a while, but they are almost invariably newcomers not yet knowing how to comport themselves effectively.

Veteran members of Congress affiliated with both parties become rich in knowledge of the government as a result of this process of constant inquiry. Some concentrate their attention on one or two agencies especially important to their constituencies or offering them personally, because of committee assignments, opportunities to achieve leadership. Senator Hayden, as an example, for many years was the Senate authority on highways and western water problems. Congress as a body thus becomes much more generally and intimately acquainted with the government than any other body, group, or interest. The Appropriations Committee's veteran members are always outstanding examples; Democrats or Republicans, they know a vast deal about the government, and understand it to an extraordinary degree—especially in its domestic aspects.

Officials involved in national defense have much to learn about secrecy from officials in departments more accustomed to dealing with a wide public while still retaining responsibility. But the vital nature of defense has made the handling of information in that area of government both difficult and exceptionally inadequate. In general, however, and especially for all other fields, the members of Congress have felt themselves satisfactorily served in terms of their information needs.

The legislators, therefore, are especially well situated to appraise, to sift out, and to experiment with particular items in terms of possible public concern. What members of Congress do not feel worth experimenting with in the arena of public discussion, the citizen is not often likely to be in need of knowing about. And of course only a part of what is proposed to public attention by members of Congress can arouse or sustain that attention.

At the state and local levels of government, the same kind of inquiry by legislators is rarely carried on. Al Smith is still legendary in New York as an assemblyman who was tireless in his study and scrutiny of the government of the state. Most of his successors spend little time in similar application, and quickly tire. Indeed, as a normal thing in most state and local governments there is little equally substantial legislative competence of the sort described above. The national government usually is more clearly a challenge, and attracts persons of much higher competence and greater maturity. But an important cause of the difference is to be found in the absence from most state and local jurisdictions of true two-party government. This is probably associated with the relative ease with which key leaders of ruling majorities may be influenced by large private interests, sometimes by means of gifts or "retainers."

No other large government in the world has so many close communications to and from so large a proportion of its citizens as does our national government. Aside from association in the familiar matters of mail service and tax collection, citizens each year enter into tens of millions of contractual relationships with the national government, make millions of calls in local, district, regional, and national offices of governmental establishments, write millions of letters and make millions of telephone calls to public servants. No other organization of any kind is known to approach such extensive relationships with people. Hospitality to such communication is very great among national officials. The obligation to communicate is keenly, if not uniformly, felt.

In very large part, although not exclusively, the most important role of the mass communication media—press, radio, and television—is auxiliary and subsequent to the interaction within the parts of government and party organizations wherever the latter are effective. In the next chapter, therefore, we give consideration to the press as illustrative of the mass media.

X

Reading the Papers

T. S. MATTHEWS, a distinguished journalist who now lives in London but who spent one decade of his career as a top editor of *Time,* has likened the press to the banks *(Sugar Pill,* New York: Simon & Schuster, 1959). Remarking how incurious many bankers are about the real nature of money, and how unclear they are about it, he has compared them with journalists similarly incurious about the real nature of news and just as unclear about it. He has gone on to say that both, to a great extent, manufacture their own product: "By far the greatest part of the world's 'money' is issued by the banks in the form of credit. Most of the world's 'news' is manufactured by the press itself."

In illustration of his point, Matthews mentioned having once examined the front page of a good American newspaper in these terms. He found that of the eleven stories on the page, seven had not happened at all. Saying that some of the many speculations about the future might have come true later on, but at the time of publication they were just speculations, he pointed up his general conclusions thus: "If news is what happened yesterday, the newspapers print an awful lot of phony news."

Is the News True?

In press dealings with government and political figures the latitude is very broad. Anyone who serves, or attempts to serve, in a government post is especially subject to critical attention, and this is most constantly and emphatically true about those in or seeking elective office. A public career is like a book, freely subject to critical review. When certain persons say something highly critical of their political opponents it is treated as news. That the statement was made is true; but the statement made is a matter of opinion, not demonstrated fact, and it is as likely as not to be a view held only by a small minority or even by only the single individual quoted.

Seeking out the unusually critical person who is willing to be quoted is one part of the news-manufacturing process. Speculation about what might conceivably happen is another and larger part, as Matthews indicated. Another part is the inflation of the ordinary, the obvious, and the conventional with headlines appearing to make news out of non-news. An example was the story emblazoned under front-page, eight-column headlines across the country in December, 1959, "Nixon Refuses To Pick Running-Mate." At that stage of the presidential campaign no one not completely insane would have done otherwise.

Most persons do not read with a keen eye for the precise phrasing which attributes a statement to somebody other than the newspaper, nor do they know how to judge the knowledge, good sense, and influence of the person or "source" quoted. They are inclined to accept the pink-pill magnate as a great authority on public policy on the thoroughly unsound ground that otherwise the paper would not quote him. They usually do not distinguish speculation about what might happen from statements about what has happened.

Most readers do not have the knowledge that enables them to discount a story about some political controversy which is nothing but a repetition of the position of a chronic dissenter, fully anticipated by his colleagues and without influence on them. They do not readily observe the use of the passive voice which a professional writer in the *Saturday Review* correctly said is "a sign that the reporters and commentators are in trouble." When the story states that a certain happening "was regarded as significant" it means that a big story has been made out of a little story, and that the passive voice has been used to inflate it and also, perhaps, as a simple hedge against the remote possibility that the reported event just might sometime come to have some degree of significance.

Newspaper readers, somewhat similarly, are not likely to be aware of the lack of relevant capacity of the local reporter who interviewed the official from Washington and was unable to ask him a sensible or useful question. They have little way of knowing that the questions asked of public men in television interviews by leading journalists often could not be answered sensibly by anyone, and could not really matter less, anyhow. In other instances they ask old, worn-out questions, eliciting old and worn-out clichés as answers.

Most readers will not weigh the fact that newspapers, like other institutions, keep utilizing the products of has-beens, either for humane reasons or because of the notion that they have large followings. Readers for the most part will not discriminate between different writers, different papers, between unsigned and signed stories, between news reports and the special "columns." Nor do readers generally recognize that journalistic success hinges much less on factual reporting and depth of insights than on ability to write interestingly.

Conscious and outright dishonesty among newspaper reporters is rare. What most of them write is true for each other, in the subtle terms of their trade. Most of it is not true for most readers in the meaning these readers give to the word "truth." Most of it is not true in terms of citizen capacity to read critically and to relate what they read to their responsibilities as citizens. The newspapers give to citizens, in figurative terms, a very, very long and confusing ballot.

It never has been possible for newspaper writers to be wholly "objective," and thus to deal exclusively with indisputable "facts." Being human, no two of them will see exactly the same things or agree precisely about what they have seen. The very sober attempt to confine reporting to objective news came to its greatest development under Melville Stone's influence in the early years of the Associated Press. It still has a certain important vitality, but the newspapers now frankly print gossip columns of various kinds, some comic strips have become propaganda media, editorial opinion columns have numerous columnist competitors ranging from specialists in sports, the theater, movies, radio, television, palmistry, teen-agers, dieting, and astrology, to books, education, health, business, and government. There are also "interpretive" news stories and there is a fairly wide range for almost any signed story. Altogether, markets, box scores, league standings, death notices, and a few other features of a similar nature aside, the more or less clearly factual material accounts for a very small part of the column inches of even the most serious newspaper of today.

Yet advertisers do not select the news as they may select and dominate the radio and television programs they "sponsor." Even the indirect influence of advertisers cannot be regarded as effective on most of the large newspapers, and resistance to intrusion on editorial responsibility has sometimes been heroic. The average intelligence of journalists is high, most of them are conscientious, and usually they have a dedication to their craft, and a belief in its social importance. With many of them, as Matthews has indicated in his book cited earlier, this sense of the social significance of their work is a fuzzy, abstract attitude that expresses itself in some oversimplified and sometimes wholly unwarranted assumptions which lead to an unhappy inflation of news. Yet newspaper folk as a whole are as self-critical as any other functional group—lawyers, doctors, churchmen, teachers, businessmen, farmers, labor leaders, politicians, or civil servants, all of whom are generally otherwise engaged.

In any field of legitimate endeavor, persons or organs in it range from excellent to poor. There are various newspaper audiences or "markets," various interpretations of "news," differences in standards of performance, and differences in policies and social attitudes. It is probably a fair generalization that the ablest political writers deal with the national and international scenes, and that the poorest governmental coverage is at the local level, with state reporting falling somewhere in between. It is also probably a fair statement that the freest perceptions and most uncomplicated patriotism are demonstrated in journalistic dealing with the international scene.

However, it is true that the search for controversy caused some leading correspondents at the end-of-war Dumbarton Oaks conference to say to United States officials, "We're not interested in knowing about agreements reached; tell us when there is disagreement." In an opposite way, as James Reston of the *New York Times* suggested before a congressional subcommittee in November, 1955, there was a conscious effort to give an optimistic flavor to reports of the Geneva Conference. How much the contradictory results were attributable to "news management" by officials in the Eisenhower administration, how much to a press bias for the one administration and against the other, and how much to conventional news practices, it would be impossible to say. Yet surely all of these elements entered into the two situations. The attitude of some of the correspondents at Dumbarton Oaks made development of the United Nations more difficult. The unwarranted optimism at Geneva built hopes destined to collapse and, collapsing, to stimulate the growth of cynicism and misunderstanding.

Woodrow Wilson had been persuaded by the time of the Versailles Conference to sponsor exposure of those important deliberations to a close and constant scrutiny of an unprecedented sort, and thus to initiate a frustrating and dangerous pattern. But the *New York Times* in 1959 applauded Mr. Hammarskjold's reply to reporters' questions, "Private talks are private talks." It had similarly applauded his statements a year earlier that the "legislative process in the United Nations is not a substitute for diplomacy" and that "the best results of negotiation between two parties cannot be achieved . . . in the full glare of publicity." Miss Pauline Frederick, as president of the U.N. Correspondents' Association, made extraordinarily responsible and discerning arguments for freeing international conferences of the pressures coming from excited headlines. But these are not the sentiments of the rank and file; the *New York Times* editorial would not have been agreed to by all its correspondents or news editors.

At the national level the London *Times* has taken high ground, emphasizing constitutional and legal bases for the oath binding Cabinet members to secrecy in the British government. It would be extremely difficult to find an equivalent example in an American paper. It is to be recognized that in simple honesty, in industry, and in the quality for which there is no better term than "patriotism," many reporters and newsdesk editors rate high. It goes without saying that they also excel most others in skill in writing interestingly for mass audiences. Principal occasions for concern go well beyond these simple virtues.

Grains of Salt on Newspaper Tales

For citizens generally, some words of warning may be offered in a simplified sequence without extended discussion. Thereafter, a few points will be considered at more length.

1. First of all, the citizen should remember that newspapers are business concerns. While there is nothing disreputable about this, and subsidized newspapers with no need to show a profit generally have not been either vital or effective, any business does rest primarily on a self-interest not synonymous with the public interest. The business of newspapers is a dual one, with two principal sources of income. It is most clearly, of course, a sales-promotion facility for the economy at large. In this function it somewhat resembles a union station which is a facility mutually useful to competing railways. In the case of the union station the public appeal is wholly in terms of serving customers. There is in the same way a public appeal in newspaper advertising, which has considerable "reader interest." In addition, the newspaper enhances reader appeal and service to advertisers by conducting apart from the advertising columns what may well be described as primarily an entertainment business. In this function it both draws much upon and builds up other great entertainment businesses—the movies, television, the theater, professional sports, recreation and resort industries. It is very much closer kin to dramatics and sports than to education, and more nearly kin to education than to direct and responsible participation in the decision-making essential to the conduct of governmental institutions.

2. Any business, or any specialized function, imposes upon those engaged in it a certain discipline, a certain loyalty, and a special preoccupation different from those imposed upon persons engaged in other functions. There is at least some real virtue in most careers, and for any particular job this is most likely to become vivid when one has that job and earns status and income from it. To some extent the best of us take home with our pay

checks a special and limited point of view. Often this results in an unconscious rationalization justifying a kind of attitude or conduct which might seem open to question when observed in someone else in another functional setting.

3. The great increase in literacy central to the unprecedented improvement in living standards in this country in recent decades opened up to the press and to advertisers new mass markets. The speed of the whole phenomenon has unquestionably handicapped the process of individual and social maturation. The average state of culture of those who read has dropped, and the level of what is actually read has been lowered as the number of those who read *something* has been greatly increased. Skills in writing and depicting things for the newly literate have been developed as principal resources of journalists and their numerous half brothers—the public relations and advertising professionals. Nurturing and deferring to mediocrity through journalism and sales promotion is a matter for grave concern. It is closely related to Walter Lippmann's worry about excessive mass dominance over political "leaders."

4. The mass orientation of the "mass media" is almost wholly reflected in matters of taste; mass "reader interest" is more sought after than the interest of the masses who read. In social and economic policy the orientation is heavily toward the privileged and toward commerce.

At the turn of the century great papers were being built as outright advocates of the underprivileged. E. W. Scripps was a great figure in that kind of building, and Joseph Pulitzer left a living monument in the *St. Louis Post-Dispatch*. But as a general thing when these builders became wealthy, and almost invariably when they died, the papers became more and more tied to the economic interests of their owners.

5. The great and rapid social and economic developments of recent decades have strained publishers' capacities of maturation along with those of the rest of us, and in any case journalists cannot be responsible for everything. Nevertheless, it is true that the very fact of becoming "mass media" made newspaper publishing very big business. It put editors and top reporters among the socially and economically privileged. There are among the papers

of large circulation hardly more than a half dozen that reflect in contemporary terms any special mass-interest preoccupation. There are more that uphold tolerance in a significant way, and a still larger number who, in newly enlightened patriotism, view the various peoples around the world as one body.

Almost any newspaper welcomes a story of some unfortunate individual whose plight arouses human sentiments; by publicizing the details the paper facilitates individual benevolence in special cases to which citizens contribute according to their generosity rather than according to their wealth. The individual case is a "story," and the story is the focus of the press. Systematic and equitable welfare arrangements by public agencies are not "stories," and often are tacitly opposed as steps toward the "welfare state." Obviously the reader cannot depend upon newspapers as a source from which he can develop social-value judgments.

The syndicated columnists constitute a special order of editorial writers. A good many of them are, like the reporters, hard workers, but I have seen a significant number shift viewpoints to make their products acceptable to publishers. In most papers there is some variety in the attitudes of columnists, in order to give a suggestion of impartiality, and an occasional star column is used because of its reader interest. But the policy range of columns is rather narrow, and their median position on domestic matters is well to the "right of center." The views of many reporters who work full time in observation of government and know most about it, privately differ so sharply from the editorial-page view as to be highly indicative of publisher dominance in the latter. Most citizens in other callings may act similarly in support of their own self-interests, but their pretensions to public responsibility are not the same.

6. American newspapers in recent decades have tended to become a one-party element. In 1944, we find, 60 per cent of the country's daily papers, with 68.5 per cent of the total circulation, were for Dewey. Twenty-two per cent of them, with 17 per cent of the circulation, were for Roosevelt. In 1948 the daily papers editorially supporting Truman constituted 15 per cent of all dailies in the country, with 10 per cent of the total circulation. In 1952 those supporting Stevenson comprised 15 per cent of the dailies.

In 1956 he again had the support of 15 per cent.* Yet in spite of the publishers' rather solid and passionate uniformity of party adherence, their papers have treated parties and their functions with little understanding or respect. Perhaps their most specific political influence has been their contribution to the extensive and misguided growth of popular pride in "voting for the man."

7. To a significant extent the press effort to secure unlimited access to governmental news-in-the-making is to be regarded as a special-interest drive. It tends to subordinate the public interest to the publishing interest. Some of the arguments are similar to Charles Wilson's famous blooper, "What is good for the country is good for General Motors and *vice versa*." Special interests are legitimate, of course, but sound public policy can be achieved only by considering any one of them along with a great many others. The newspapers are in a position to give influential precedence to their own special interest in governmental news. This fact somewhat offsets the mild distinction which might be made between the special interest of reporters and the special interest of lobbyists seeking, say, increased subsidies for the merchant marine. The pursuit of stories that will increase circulation of the papers is a little less exclusively, directly, and consciously an effort to secure monetary gain than is the lobbying effort.

8. Special interests tend to rest their cases on some general dicta offered as axioms automatically serving the public interest. Press advocates have often asserted, for instance, that "the more news about government, the better it is for all citizens." It may be similarly supposed that the biggest high chair is the best high chair for any baby, or that the biggest shoes are preferable to shoes that fit you; or that confusion is better than enlightenment. Two things are certain. One is that poppycock is poppycock, whether oral or printed. The second is that there is no demonstrated relationship between the number of column inches read about government, and outstanding citizenship or governmental understanding. Justice Holmes was a competent citizen during the years when he read no newspapers and only one periodical dealing at all with public affairs.

*The data were gathered by the newspapers' principal trade journal, *Editor and Publisher,* and recapitulated in its issue of Nov. 3, 1956.

9. All functions develop patterns of workways which become conventional and continue to be accepted without much critical attention. In the case of the press there are several such features that are worth examining. One is the "scoop" convention—the premium put upon getting news first. This has been stretched into a competition in speculation, through news that in a factual sense is not news at all but which greatly misinforms and confuses the public. Speculation provides the prime refutation of the "gospel" phrase, "the more news, the better." This convention will be given further consideration later in this chapter.

Another important convention, of course, is the one of periodicity—a daily newspaper requires daily flows of news, columns, headlines, and related matter. Inevitably much of the flow becomes triviality, repetition, and "news" inflation.

A third convention which leads to great public misunderstanding lies in the set of assumptions and practices governing news headlines. The general rule is roughly that the headlines must make a statement of news fact in the present tense; headlines for any particular paper must conform to a systematic pattern of type sizes, mass and structure in number of lines, "decks," and length of lines in decks. The result striven for is to make interesting-looking pages, more or less symmetrical in a certain complex sense, with quickly identifiable headlines which are attention-compelling.

These are incidental, typographical, and attention-catching requirements, and, enmeshed by the convention, newspaper folk are likely to forget that, to the public, headlines are the most insistent of all the things the newspapers "say." Yet the frequency with which these headlines say things not said in the stories beneath them is fairly high, and the frequency with which they give an impression which is not the real summation of the stories underneath is very high. Even if the headline writers had more time than the publication deadlines permit, they could not possibly put into them what the stories contain. If they could, it would be a devastating indictment of the succeeding paragraphs. Yet there is hardly ever any conscious effort to mislead. Nor does there seem to be any available reform. Readers should—but are hardly likely to—simply recognize headlines as categorizing labels.

There is finally the convention of "drama" as the most common focus of reader interest. Most reporters spend a good many man-years prospecting for conflict, and actually manufacturing it. This pursuit is associated with their own incidental desire to play safe in the event that an interesting conflict does in fact develop. Altogether, the result is to accelerate almost any things, persons, or phenomena that show signs of mobility.

10. The responsible decision-makers have shown no inclination to get answers to their problems from the journalists. That particular things are printed means that they have been added to other "political facts"; for this reason—not so much because of their intrinsic content—officials need to know about them. And officials need to be most considerate of journalists. But the experience and responsibilities of journalists are not directly transmutable into decisions about the conduct of public institutions.

"Scoops"

When the "scoop" idea was new it had reference to getting into print faster than the opposition a report of some actual happening. Happenstance in location, skill at telegraphy, ingenuity in tying up lines of communication, or success in a kind of detective work were some of the possible elements of a news beat. More and more systematization of news arrangements, and the relative rarity of factual news beats, seem to have contributed to a great shift to a type of story in which the reporter has tried to deduce or guess something of the future course of events. For example, the number of column inches printed in daily papers guessing at how budgetary formulations will shape up at the end of a fiscal year is many times more than the number of column inches printed after-the-fact about the figures as they actually developed. Citizens who discuss such matters, consequently, spend much more time and energy dealing with inaccurate information than they do with the facts.

The press practice about speculative news differs according to level of government, branch of government, and functions. The papers tend to speculate most about the national government, there to confine themselves in their speculations principally to the executive branch, secondarily to the legislative branch, and hardly at all to the judiciary, insofar as the actual decision-making process is involved.

Within the executive government, speculation is restrained in news dealing with national defense. Some of this restraint is voluntary because of the journalists' special sense of responsibility altogether appropriate in matters relating to national security. Some of the restraint is a consequence of official classification of the material. Material classified is more voluminous than its content warrants, and classification is often continued for too long a time, although no one would deny that some restriction is required because of damage the nation might otherwise sustain. But the fact remains that national defense is the only extensive national governmental area in which secrecy much obtains after decision or action. Generally, access to information after decision within the executive branch is much more useful to citizens than premature or speculative material.

However, except for matters concerning national security, many members of the press regard all stages of all governmental executive work as a domain that should be wide open to the press. The reporters' acquaintance with stenographers, knowledge of the grievances of unhappy subordinates, social associations of many kinds, and sheer "power of the press" facilitate deep penetration of the executive establishments. Such aggressive intrusion can impair responsibility, breed timidity, discourage full official consideration of policy problems, overload and mislead citizens with "news."

It is a common reportorial practice to glean from some person well below the level where a particular decision will be made this person's notion of a possible line of action, and to print that as a speculative possibility. This may be something that would never actually be seriously considered at a higher level, but its publication can cause higher officials—and citizens—to spend much time and energy wastefully dealing with the consequences of that "news" story. Another type of speculative news is a story guessing the "original authors" of certain kinds of policy. More often than not there is no particular author, because the decision was the distilled wisdom of a responsible institutional organ. In any case, authorship would have no public significance. For citizens the proper question is, "Who was the highest ranking person who approved it?" or, "Who is responsible for rectification?" Present journalistic practice encourages citizens to hunt for responsibilities exercised by underlings they never can or should, in fact, identify. This is an effort to carry the long ballot to the nth degree, putting innumerable problems on citizen shoulders, and it causes everybody to wind up in guesswork.

Executive decisions are usually particular ones within the bounds of general policies already publicly explored and arrived at by Congress or to be submitted to Congress. They are the daily occupation of thousands of persons who can be personally known to only a few citizens and whose whole careers may be easily ruined by any kind of publicity, printed or oral. They feel weak, and are weak, before journalists, members of Congress, party leaders, and pressure groups. The decisions they make are made by an intricate process of inter- and intra-institutional interactions among many persons with different backgrounds and abilities. These "decisions" are usually decisions to recommend; if they are more than that they are all made under the direction of a series of top political officers. The proper service of executive rank and file is essentially intra-institutional, and higher-ups should be held accountable for the actions taken by the institutions they head. Higher-ups, similarly, should be the channels of communication with press, legislators, and large pressure groups. In the executive branch, attention of the press can be most useful when it is directed toward needed correction of actions already taken.

Legislators, on the other hand, are higher-ups. Their decisions are usually major or basic ones (at least outside the field of foreign affairs), and less easily and quickly to be changed than most executive decisions of similar importance. Their function is one broadly appropriate to kleig lights, although they have recourse to relative privacy when they need it. In general, their public performance and their interpretation of the public reaction to it are of the essence of their function. They are where they are by virtue of popular action; they are readily identified and seek identification. They are personages; they are generally tough, competent in political warfare and skilled in self-defense. The legislative process is relatively easy for citizens to understand, and it is not often that a legislator feels the process has been impaired by journalistic enterprise or speculative news.

The press shows little inclination to attribute responsibility for congressional action to office or committee staff personnel, even though these employees inevitably have real influence. It has been asserted that a committee staff worker inserted in the bill authorizing government loans to students the double-oath provision which later became a subject of national controversy. The insertion is believed to have been made without the knowledge of the committee. Congress probably would not knowingly have required the second oath, but found it troublesome to amend the statute. The press properly made little of this staff member's action: the responsibility rested with Congress.

The contrast between press habits and working situations in the executive and legislative branches just suggested is a significant one. The chief handicap to legislative performance resulting from journalistic activity is one in which individual members of Congress and the weakness of party discipline are chiefly at fault. This handicap arises from the mere availability of a medium in which members of the legislature may carry on—and are insistently invited to carry on—an excessively individualistic performance. The maverick, the eccentric, and the demagogue get the headlines. This fuzzes over party responsibility, lowers the quality of public performance, and impairs the public's capacity to hold officials accountable.

The courts, in sharper contrast, are given radically more respectful treatment by the press than either of the other two branches. Any one of the high courts where more than one judge sits offers a decision-making situation in which there are untouched dramatic possibilities. Within such courts there must be give-and-take in the process of arriving at a group judgment, and the decisions are heavy laden with public interest. Yet reporters do not constantly and impudently speculate about forthcoming decisions, nor scuttle about trying to get hints about what Justice Blank has said to Justice Mount, or cultivate the justices' secretaries socially to that end, or browbeat the justices before television audiences. Freedom of the press is felt to be unimpaired so long as comment may be untrammeled *after* the actual rendering of an opinion.

How much of this difference in reportorial and editorial attitudes is attributable to the influence of ubiquitous lawyers in achieving a sort of sanctification of their own functional temples, how much to belief in functional differences between the judicial and other branches, and how much to the courts' power to punish for contempt, it would be hard to say. Not only is it true that speculation about prospective court decisions hardly ever appears, however; it is also true that the only reportorial demand for fuller access to court news is to the formal court sessions normally open to the public. Closed hearings of the kind challenged by the press are by far most numerous at local levels of government, although not unknown at the level of United States district courts. As now handled by the press, news of higher courts is more manageable by citizens and serves citizen needs better than news of the executive branch, and at least moderately better than news of legislative bodies.

The Fourth Estate Myth

The worst result of modern news-handling relates to the executive branch and derives from the "scoop" convention. The search for premature news tends to incite frantic decision making by officials, in terms of beating somebody else to the news punch, in terms of being in the news often, or in terms of answering a question at the moment simply because some correspondent has asked it. An able journalist, Douglas Cater, in his admirable book, *The Fourth Branch of Government* (Boston: Houghton Mifflin Co., 1959), tells of an illustrative case in which our conduct of foreign policy was damaged by an acting secretary of state when he yielded too quickly to the insistent press importunity for a statement on a particular matter. I have seen similar things happen on scores of occasions. Weak officials must be given major blame for such irresponsible disregard of the public interest. If the press is absolved of blame, however, it must relinquish claims to being a "fourth estate," or a fourth branch of government. The title of Cater's book was used only as a headline.

Of course the press is not in fact a fourth branch of government. Cater himself approvingly quoted Arthur Krock of the *New York Times* as summing up "succinctly the conflicting mandates of newspaperman and official." Krock had said that for the newspaperman the questions are few and simple: Is it true? Has it been legitimately acquired? Is it fit to print—public property or a private matter? Krock had gone on to list some of the other considerations the statesman must have: Is it premature: Will publication make the going more difficult? Will publication tend to confuse, rather than to clarify, the popular mind?

To the newspaper man the story is the primary consideration. To the official the objectives are to develop the best possible policy and to enunciate it in the most useful way. Responsibilities are extremely unlike. The press is not a fourth branch of government because its top executives are not subject to eviction by impeachment, by political executives, or by popular vote at intervals not far apart. It is no more a branch of government than any other entity which has a private interest to promote through the use of government information. Its function is not governance, whatever else it may be, and it is not accountable for governance.

The natural preoccupation of newspaper folk with their own work results in a tendency on their part to overlook the resources and activities of Congress and the opposition party in respect to critical scrutiny of basic governmental organs.

The capacity of the Congress to know about and to appraise what is being done in the executive branch is vastly more impressive as well as more responsible than the related capacity of the press. Cater has pointed out in this connection how in Britain the questions reporters would ask here are asked by "elected Members of Parliament who are politicians long trained in the art of government [who] may one day be on the other side. Thus questions, though perhaps highly partisan, are generally responsible." Cater then observes that in Washington the questioning is conducted according to the reporter's concept of what is news.

While we do not have and should not have here the parliamentary system of Britain, we could do with a more clear-cut party alignment in Congress. But even now the members of Congress can and do ask more good questions, and ask them more responsibly, than most correspondents have any notion of, and more than all of the correspondents together have capacity for. The members of Congress have relevant resources peculiar to themselves, back home, with their colleagues, with their staffs, and in their basic power over the bureaucracy. They ask questions day in, day out, individually, by letter, by telephone, and face to face; they also ask through staff assistants. And the questions total thousands on a typical workday. Thereby the veteran members, especially, become almost unbelievably well-informed. Congress as a whole is thoroughly informed in terms of its needs and citizen needs. Citizens may wisely reserve most of their critical attention to executive branch matters for those things about which experienced members of Congress show definite concern.

There will be in addition, of course, stories the correspondents develop from executive press releases and press conferences. Some of them will be worth the attention of particular citizens. But the citizen should be skeptical of stories pretending to present startling discoveries in the policy-making area. The story about an action taken after months of theretofore unpublicized argument and negotiation within the bureaucracy, under authority earlier explored and granted by Congress, can usually be passed over quickly in the realization that everything has been done in the national interest that could be done as of the particular moment: if a better decision is possible, the need for it will appear as we live with this one.

Citizens as News Consumers

The primary, basic function of the press in reporting government news should be, theoretically, to give the information that will help citizens decide for or against the party in power. The second basic function, similarly, should be to give party members information that will help them choose nominees. The third important function should be to give information that will help citizens decide whether to push for *changes in decisions already made* by the government. These relate to the three great powers of the citizens.

In practice, however, the press seems unlikely to be of much direct help in the first two of these citizen responsibilities. The selection of a party to support and the selection of candidates to nominate are the concerns of the political party instruments of citizens, and it is almost inevitable that mass media, simply because they are mass media, will withhold their columns from frank service of party causes. Further, the service of this particular kind of citizen need would require a great divergence from the conventional news preoccupation with daily drama, incident, and controversy for their own sakes.

It seems probable that the press will contribute most *directly* to citizen judgment most often in terms of the third basic function of citizens—agitating for improvements, reforms, and policy changes in governmental activities previously determined upon. The press is especially effective when it identifies impropriety, favoritism, or corruption. It is admirably equipped to make disclosures of authenticated actions and conditions needing public attention. Some of these matters will be failings within government, and some will be failings in society.

Questionable awards of contracts, kickbacks from employees, use of public money to pay for office rent on one's own porch, and inequitable realty assessments illustrate possibilities within the government. Used-car misrepresentation and fraud such as was revealed by the *Washington Star* in 1960, resulting in a new licensing system for dealers in the District of Columbia, illustrated similar possibilities outside of government.

In larger terms, and in general, however, the service of the press to citizens as sovereigns is chiefly significant in the long run: in the course of years, in the duration of an entire administration, or in an entire campaign; not at the moment, not in a single day, in a single story, or in a single "column," and not in panic or frenzy.

What has been said in a critical way applies to news magazines in about the same degree as to newspapers; they are roughly comparable to Sunday newspapers, but likely to be more thoroughly managed as personal organs, whether in the dignified and responsible manner of Albert Shaw in the long-dead *Review of Reviews* or in the Luce manner displayed in *Time*. News magazines seem to be the only feasible form a national newspaper can take in this extensive country.

Television news is more directly tied to advertising "messages," and is damaged by its moronic associations, but supports a few sturdy and worthy stars in the public-affairs firmament. Fundamentally, of course, radio and television news resembles newspaper news. It especially resembles headlines.

The drive of newspaper leaders for more quantity in governmental news overlooks many fundamental features of American journalism which make their effort largely irrelevant to citizen service. The misplaced emphasis on amusing or sensational or diverting trivia which will catch attention and build circulation makes profitable citizen-reading extremely difficult. Finding significant news in the midst of such non-news is even more difficult than finding the drug dispensary in the modern "drugstore."

One of the most competent newspaper readers I know told me about a hunt for important factual news in an instance unhappily not hard to duplicate. This concerned the tainted-cranberry incident. My friend lived in an area where cranberry production is important. For ten days the newspapers in the large cities in that part of the country devoted many columns to telling about the interdiction of certain cranberries by Secretary Flemming of the Department of Health, Education, and Welfare. The whole impact, bolstered by the dramatics of political figures in eating uninspected cranberries, was an imputation of idiocy on the part of the bureaucracy. My friend read assiduously in an effort to find out the reason for Secretary Flemming's action. He got an incomplete idea about it in one Sunday feature after a week, when most citizens had quit reading about the matter, their opinions already made. But a rounded view he got only in the *Manchester* (England) *Guardian* still later.

Even when the actual reporting is more defensible, there is serious reason to question its serviceability. Bruce Bliven, as an eminent journalist guest editorial writer in the June 11, 1960, issue of the *Saturday Evening Post* said: "America boasts that it is the land of superlative mass communication. Never in history have so many people been told so much, in such a variety of ways. Somehow the messages seem to miss the target." Dean Edward Barrett of the Columbia University School of Journalism, in a report on journalism education published about the same time, said that "the thoughtful citizen who seeks to be reasonably informed must make extraordinary efforts to do so." He might have added that many citizens are inadequately equipped to exercise the discrimination in selection and evaluation of news that is necessary to that end.

A friend who is exceptionally well-informed about government has remarked to me in all seriousness that on a number of occasions inability to read the papers for as long as six months resulted in missing nothing significant except a few obituaries. I have had a similar experience while on duty abroad. I have missed some interesting news, but nothing important to me as a citizen.

I do not mean to suggest that responsible citizens should not read the papers. I do mean that they should read them skeptically, as selectively as possible, and otherwise in a highly relaxed mood, suspending judgment while waiting for further and more reliable information than is contained in one day's paper. Most questions from other newspaper readers about one's opinion concerning this or that story in the day's news are not worth uttering or answering.

Professional press comment should be heavily discounted for the same reasons; for the most part, if read a decade later most of these old comments would be amusing, or wholly devoid of interest, if not so distressingly lacking in significance. A rare column stands up. And once in a while, even at the time of publication, a gem appears from a slightly peripheral source. An example of the latter sort was an article in *The New Yorker* of June 18, 1960, by E. B. White. Mr. White writes about public affairs only rarely, after he has had time to get perspective and to think. Newspaper subscribers would do well to read their papers in the same unfevered way.

If a survey were to be taken, the United States, with the high average number of newspapers read by the typical citizen, with all the millions of copies of news magazines, with the greatest numbers of radio and television news programs and listeners, certainly would be shown to be almost immeasurably far in front in terms of quantity of governmental news available and consumed. It is likely that the political unhappiness and confusion here also rate at the top among democratic peoples in advanced nations.

There have been a great many small studies which show that amazingly few people know the names of more than a handful of political leaders and holders of public office. This is all the more devastating in the face of the extent of an ill-founded moral pride in "voting for the man, not the party." And the most voluminous newspaper grist is "news" about personalities.

Certainly it is not the amount of news available nor the extent of news gluttony among citizens, that is the crowning and saving glory of a democratic society. There are many important questions about kind, timing, and manner of news presentation—in terms of citizen utilization of news—which journalists generally avoid.

Happily, there are millions whose understanding of government is not primarily dependent upon their gleanings from the current affairs press. There are hundreds of thousands of immigrants and first-generation residents who have a perspective enabling them to appreciate and react to the government with unusual understanding. There are millions of citizens who work now, and other millions who have worked, for the government, for periods long enough and with attitudes open enough to permit a great enrichment of outlook. There are other millions whose insights have been derived from work with parties. Some in both categories, and some in many different situations, have had worldly experience of an especially useful sort, and an exceptional capacity to learn from it. Of these, some have first come to public eminence in the nongovernmental scene, but in their work somehow developed an especially responsible sense of public affairs. The names of Stimson, Clayton, Bunker, Hoffman, Bowles, Foster, Lovett, Harriman, and Benton are illustrative. These millions and these special few together greatly support belief in the feasibility of popular sovereignty.

XI

Public Finance

THE ENORMOUS difference between family finance and national finance has many causes and many aspects, but it begins in the fact that the power to "coin money and fix the value thereof" is exclusively vested in the national government. This fundamental function itself directly involves the government in much more than the management of coinage and currency. Most money is in neither of these two forms; it is in bank credits.

In an eighteen-year period ending in March, 1957, coins and currency available for banks and citizens increased by $19.4 billion—from $6.2 billion to $25.6 billion. In the same period, the total supply of cash, demand deposits, and savings accounts increased by $192.5 billion—from $62.9 billion to $255.4 billion.

The sovereign authority has to do with the management of the total supply of money. This is associated with a still broader responsibility for general economic order.

Fiscal management of affairs by the government altogether is a highly technical business, and it is not necessary for citizens at large to be fully acquainted with such technicalities. Use of appropriate technicians in various executive agencies of the government with interacting and competitive concerns, while the executive and legislative branches and the two partisan groups in both legislative houses jealously watch each other and argue out fiscal

157

problems, assures a highly representative determination of issues. Dependence of both congressional and executive leadership on popular acceptance also insures solutions that give great weight to popular prejudices.

Here, then, it seems unnecessary to explore numerous aspects of public finance, and desirable to concentrate attention on a few widespread misunderstandings of some of the especially important matters.

First of all, a reminder is offered that public finance is most like private finance in one small particular that for a variety of reasons seems to be generally overlooked. The similarity is in the fact that the government *spends* the money it takes in, just as does the grocer. It often seems to be assumed that the government eats or otherwise consumes or destroys the money it collects—that taxes paid represent a total loss to the economy. Actually, of course, the government is itself a great contributor to the economy, providing important elements in the standard of living. It also functions as a point of turnover of money in the way the grocery store does when it pays money out of its receipts to transportation companies, sales people, executives, jobbers, and wholesalers, who in their turn continue the process of keeping money in motion. The government pays out money in salaries to persons who spend it for innumerable goods and services; it pays out money to contractors, to bondholders, to suppliers, to other citizens as benefit payments or subsidies to business, and for countless other purposes. The recipients of the money also pay it out in a similar fashion. Everyone knows this, of course, but many seem usually to have forgotten it. The government is itself an important element in our great prosperity in this and in many other ways.

Of much more importance is the fact that the public is confused chiefly about basic matters having little resemblance to problems of family finance—the national debt, budget-balancing, inflation, and the pattern of taxation. In this chapter we shall concentrate attention on these subjects.

The National Debt

It may be helpful to approach consideration of the national debt by examining the phenomenon of private debt. In many instances it is a device for transferring property. It is often used to facilitate settlement of estates when there are several heirs. Inflation, savings, population increases, economic growth, and technological developments all contribute to a tendency for private debt to increase irregularly but on the whole continuously.

Bonds of industrial and commercial firms are, of course, a device by which money is borrowed without title fully passing. With a prior claim on *income* of the company, *title* claims are involved only in the event of delinquency. Such a highly successful concern as the American Telephone and Telegraph Company has almost steadily increased the amount of its bonds outstanding, often establishing new annual records for size of issues. While particular bonds may be called in some instances, and others are paid or refinanced as they mature, the general condition is one in which outstanding bonds increase in amount both in general and for growing companies, so that they constitute in effect a permanent growing debt, paid off only in case of liquidation.

Other private debt is represented by real estate mortgages, chattel mortgages, promissory notes with banks and other lenders, installment buying contracts, and unsecured obligations of many kinds. (In certain senses, at least, stocks in large, management-dominated corporations also resemble debt in constituting claims on the corporation's income—and on their assets if they are liquidated.) That the amount of different kinds of debt will fluctuate with changes in governing circumstances but increase altogether in the long run is shown by each year's Economic Report of the President.

Individual debt dropped from the $72.3 billion level it had reached in the late nineteen twenties to $53.0 billion in 1940 as a consequence of the depression, then rose to $238.5 billion in 1958 as a result of war, inflation, population growth, and economic advancement. Corporate debt behaved similarly, dropping from its level of $88.9 billion in 1929 to $75.6 billion in 1940, and then rising to $236.0 billion by 1958. State and local debt offset these changes in a relatively small degree during the depression, going from $13.2 billion in 1929 to $16.5 billion in 1940, and then rising steadily to $50.9 billion by 1958. The national debt similarly rose from $16.5 billion in 1929 to $44.8 billion in 1940, and with the war rose rapidly to $252.7 billion in 1945, dropping to $222.9 billion in 1952, and rising to $241.2 billion in late 1961. In total the net debt of both public and private kinds dropped from 1929 to 1932, and was still $1 billion below the 1929 figure in 1940, but increased by $567 billion between 1929 and 1958.

The matters presented in this section suggest or imply nine summarizing statements bearing upon the subject of public debt:

1. The total debt of an expanding capitalist economy grows, and should grow, at a not too irregular rate. The relationship between rates of growth in the public and private sectors is highly technical, not surely lending itself to any useful specific summation. It is clear, however, that the public crisis of war limits and directs the growth of private debt, and that public debt should increase disproportionally when the total of private debt is diminishing.

2. Without debt there would be little attractive or useful incentive to save, little vehicle for investment. To rely on 100 per cent owner-operated and debtless business would produce a kind of society unattractive to us insofar as it succeeded, and an economy incapable of sufficiently great success.

3. The total debt is related to population, capital accumulation, and the state of technology. Capital accumulation lends itself fairly readily to management and seems to proceed in a fairly orderly way. Population growth is generally unmanaged, frequently surprising. Under private enterprise, technological development is directly unmanaged; and in a large way probably at all manageable, for the most part, only by means of indirect governmental influence. It is at least potentially explosive in its expansiveness. These considerations make highly essential the kind of general, economic management for which government is peculiarly adapted, including its use of debt as one important fiscal tool.

4. Debt is one way of channeling energies according to need and opportunity.

5. Debt is a way of shifting title to properties, in particular enabling the younger generation to buy out the preceding one in an orderly fashion.

6. Debt as a whole is never paid off, even though individuals or

single enterprises may pay all indebtedness in favorable or ruinous circumstances. Debt elimination is usually associated with depression, impoverishment requiring sale of assets, liquidation, or bankruptcy.

7. For our profit-and-loss economy in general it is impossible—as well as undesirable—to meet all running expenses, to cover depreciation, offset all losses, pay interest on total investment, accumulate capital for the additional investment essential to an expanding economy, *and pay off existing investment* too.

8. The use of debt affects distribution of income within an economy, as do price structures, wage scales, tax arrangements, interest rates, patents, and other competitive conditions.

9. While the government guides the economy, it is part of it, too. Although the notion that government finances are the same as family finances is poppycock, governmental debt resembles the *generality* of private debt in that it, too, will increase somewhat irregularly but substantially so long as we remain a successful nation, even though relatively small reductions in it may be made from time to time. Paying off the national debt is, therefore, not a problem for our grandchildren.

We are leaving much more than the national debt to coming generations. We are leaving the bonds, which are assets for their owners; we are leaving the fiscal resources of a nation rapidly getting richer, technologies not developed when we were young, and much learning earlier undreamed of. Our grandchildren, as citizens, are prospectively in no worse situation than are the grandchildren of present stockholders of the American Telephone & Telegraph Company, who also face more and bigger bond issues. Even with the notable research which that company carries on, and with its very privileged situation so far as patronage is concerned, it is more likely to face obsolescence than is government. Our main problem is not the future payment of the national debt or the A. T. & T. debt: it is our continued success as a nation. As some wag has put it, the only national debt we have to pay is our obligation to Madison, Hamilton, Washington, Jefferson, Jackson, Lincoln, and our other eminent political forebears.

Lewis Kimmel, of the Brookings Institution, in a recent book, *Federal Budget and Fiscal Policy 1789-1958* (Washington: Brookiugs Institution, 1959), cited Lincoln's attitude on the national debt as it is recorded in *Messages and Papers of the Presidents*. Our debt multiplied itself thirty-four times in the Lincoln administration—much more rapidly than at any other time in our history. The interest rate reached 7½ per cent, too. This is the essential paragraph from Kimmel:

Lincoln was not greatly concerned by the rise in the federal debt. Toward the end of the war he stated that the federal debt was a species of property. "Held, as it is, for the most part by our own people, it has become a substantial branch of national, though private, property. For obvious reasons the more nearly this property can be distributed among all the people the better. . . . The great advantage of citizens being creditors as well as debtors with relation to the public debt is obvious. Men readily perceive that they cannot be much oppressed by a debt which they owe to themselves."

Along with Lincoln's common sense and strong popular support, the difficulties of financing the Civil War were met with inventiveness in the chartering of national banks and authorizing them, within prescribed limits, to deposit national bonds with the Comptroller of the Currency, continue to receive interest on the bonds, but to receive in their stead "national bank notes," good as legal tender. The banks could have some of their cake and eat it, too. These bank notes remained a feature of our currency for two decades after formation of the Federal Reserve System.

Paul Samuelson of the Massachusetts Institute of Technology has formulated some tables (*Economics,* New York: McGraw-Hill Book Co., 1958) which show fluctuations in cost of the United States and British national debts in two different terms. One table shows the debt as a percentage of the respective national incomes. The second table shows variations in the number of years or fractions of a year in which the particular national income would equal the debt of that country. The tables show, Samuelson points out, that the debt was most a "burden" in the years of Britain's greatest glory, and that the American national debt has never approached the relative significance of the British debt in terms of the worries often expressed here.

Enough has been said in this discussion to make it clear that the public debt is neither such a danger nor such a burden as many have been led to believe. The economic well-being of citizens may crucially depend at any particular time upon the government increasing its debt, with no offsetting increases in its own tangible assets. If the government, by borrowing some billions of dollars instead of raising the sum by taxation, averts a drop in national income, converts the otherwise inevitable drop into an increase in net national product, and increases the value of private assets by some additional billions, it is a course highly profitable to the society, even though "unprofitable" to the government in the short view.

When a private enterprise adds to its "funded" (long-term) debt, it usually does so in order to enlarge its properties as a means to enlargement of its business. While it increases its liabilities, it also increases its assets and its earning prospects. When government borrows it does so to increase its "earning prospects," in a sense, at least, but with no particular concern for adding to its tangible assets. It is true of some businesses that their "good will" represents more value than their tangible property, and it is true of most successful businesses that good will adds significantly to the value represented by their tangible assets. Hence even for corporations debt does not require justification by a demonstration of offsetting tangible assets.

While it would be absurd to justify the governmental debt by a demonstration of governmental assets, it will be illuminating to most citizens to learn that tangible assets of the national government do in fact, in the customary way of taking inventories, approximately equal the national debt. Those properties to which title clearly vests in the national government have been listed annually for some time by the House Committee on Government Operations.

The committee feels that donated property and other items listed at acquisition cost or "no value" result in a substantial understatement of what is in private business thought of as "true value." Nevertheless, the committee's careful report for June, 1958, shows the government's real estate to have a value of $66.7 billions. Under the heading of "personal property" the report listed $10.7 billions in cash, $3.932 billions in investments, $5.866 billions in accounts and notes receivable, $5.573 billions in commodities for sale, $18.484 billions in loans receivable. Other items, including equipment and supplies, bring the total of personal property to $195.348 billion, and the total assets of all kinds to $262.056 billion. It is clear that the actual property owned by the national government has, in conventional inventory and balance-sheet terms, a value approximately equal to the national debt.

There are some related items that deserve mention. The national government has an investment in highways having a current value of billions, but owned by subordinate units of government. The government has investments in, but no title to, a good many parks, schools, hospitals, and other important state or local government property items. The government owns what in other circumstances would be called a franchise for the coining of money. The annual profit on this franchise, if capitalized, would justify a valuation of some $5 billion. The Federal Reserve System is legally owned by its member banks, but their profit in it is limited and the government can be said to have an important, though somewhat informal and altogether residual, interest in the System. Since the System has paid the government an average of $362 million a year for the last five years reported at the time this is written, this theoretical equity may be conservatively valued at no less than $4 billion.

Altogether, it should be agreed that the government itself has a very good balance sheet. More importantly, it deserves a significant share of the credit for the history-shattering balance sheet which can be drawn up for the huge private economy.

Budget Balancing

The function of budget staffs in almost all kinds of organizations is chiefly managerial and money saving. In the process, the budget organization influences the determination of relative emphasis to be given to each of numerous programs. In seeking economy and in participating in the choice of spending targets it has to do with fiscal policy.

The staff in the Budget Bureau in Washington is complemented by similar staffs with more specialized responsibilities in departments and bureaus. In the administratively advanced states and larger local jurisdictions there is a pattern of much the same sort. Where the function is strongest the total number of persons engaged in this work constitutes one-fifth of 1 per cent, or less, of all personnel in that level of government. This small body of craftsmen has the principal responsibility for a rather strictly negative approach to government programs.

There are other managerial staffs, such as those in the personnel field, and there are many persons in government as well as outside who are economy-minded. But in a rough way it may be said that people not in these special managerial posts are generally on the expansive side. I have seen a good many instances in which the inventive ingenuity of government personnel had labor-saving, cost-reducing consequences, but the needs laid before government employees by citizens more often stimulate them to see new ways to be helpful, new ways to spend money for the public good.

In the instance of the snow survey, invented to give farmers in western irrigated areas a basis for planning their production programs, the work was a slight addition to tasks already performed by persons in several different bureaus of two departments, and the total additional annual cost for a result of great value was about a hundred dollars. But in other cases, as when specialists in agricultural engineering, soils, agronomy, and geography began concurrently to see the need for new efforts in soil conservation, a whole new profession and an extensive public-service program resulted.

A great deal of the drive of programmatic personnel, however, is less inventive, pointed simply toward the getting of more funds to do more of what in at least a similar fashion is already being done. The military people are in this, perhaps, especially illustrative because of the need they see to keep up with potential enemies and because of the difficulty of knowing how soon some military methods and instruments are in fact obsolete. The tendency, therefore, is to carry on the cavalry, say, when tanks are already prominently in the picture.

This kind of drive is quite different from the empire-building ambition often attributed to the bureaucrats. In my observation the empire-builder type is rather rarer in government than elsewhere, and rare anywhere. In government, to build an empire means to increase one's responsibility, and governmental responsibility weighs heavily on almost any shoulders. The drive for enlargement is rather an effort to do a better job. The distinction is thin, but it has real meaning. In any case, these drives to do more of the same are the ones most readily, even though still with much difficulty, addressed by budget staffs.

The drive that is more distinctly in pursuit of a new idea may come, as already suggested, from the civil servants in a particular programmatic or administrative area. It poses no great problem for the budgeteers, however, unless it is supported by political heads of agencies. New programmatic undertakings are determined upon in their largest dimensions and most novel character in the citadels of political leadership by departments heads, chief executive, and legislative leadership. No government will defer to budgetary units when a declaration of war is under consideration, or when a large new domestic program is being proposed to ameliorate substantial citizen distress or to serve a vivid national need.

After the major policy decisions are made, the budget staff may and does engage in "whittling" expenditures and influencing operations in the direction of refinement of effort. In this, they have the strongest support of most of the same political leadership that had agreed to the expansive programs. In the case of modern war, such whittling may involve billions of dollars without any actual impairment of the war effort. And it is in connection with this general review and pressure on program agencies that the budget-balancing objectives are most constantly pursued. In this phase, there is some concert of effort on the part of budget and managerial staffs throughout the government.

The balancing of the budget may be thought of in terms of each fiscal year, or in terms of an economic cycle or portion of a cycle. If we knew certainly there would be three years of heavy unemployment and declining prices, and that by automatic counterpoise there would then be three years of full employment and rising prices, we might all readily agree to an unbalancing of the budget for three years. We might so agree, understanding that the deficits of the first three years would be rather exactly offset by surpluses in the three following years. Cycles have no such symmetry in either time or intensity, but some such thinking began to be orthodox at least as early as the recommendations sponsored by Herbert Hoover when he was Secretary of Commerce. This entailed abandonment of the exclusive consideration of national budgets in terms of single fiscal years.

Practice went further faster than conscious changes in theory. Public need weighed more heavily than addiction to a budget-balancing theory, even though several years might be allowed for the balancing to be achieved. Still believing in the theory of an eventual balance between deficits and surpluses, decision-makers began to do what they thought desirable and feasible in the public interest and postponed consideration of budgetary theory.

This had long been the responsible attitude in time of war, of course. Most of the large national debts heretofore accumulated have been related to national defense. But the great depression constituted an equivalent crisis, and it was then that practice mildly subordinated budget balancing to the meeting of non-military crisis. It was several years before new theory began to rationalize the practice, for social theory is primarily an attempted description of reality. But before dealing with newer theory, let us glance at past wartime practice.

Reference to Civil War financing was made in a preceding section of this chapter. In the World War I period the British debt was multiplied 11 times, and the United States debt was multiplied 19.5 times. The British debt increased only about three-fold in the World War II period, while the United States debt was multiplied 5.8 times between 1939 and 1957.

Higher tax rates were more quickly established in both nations for World War II purposes, and economic controls of other sorts were more quickly and effectively instituted. These things reflected both governmental and popular learning from World

War I experience. They were caused also by a heightened sense of urgency associated with the greater threat attributable to new technological capacities of the enemy. (In both wars Britain taxed relatively more and imposed tighter controls than did the United States, because of closer and more complete physical involvement in the conflict.)

All of the *real* costs of war are actually paid, of course, during the war; guns do not exist that have not been paid for in essential terms. The question of *who* is to pay, and how much, however, is characteristically deferred. Wartime deficits are largely incurred as a way—while meeting the tragedy of war itself—of avoiding the political shock and economic disorder that would be involved in a full and immediate facing of this question: Who is to pay how much? In other words, deficits—and inflation—in wartime help prevent adverse effects on incentives both to work and to save. Economists call this the "money illusion," referring to the fact that persons react according to money income and prices without fully realizing that their real incomes are not behaving in the same way, or at least not to the same extent, as their money incomes.

Deficits, then, may be seen as serving to defer and diffuse the *ultimate incidence* of some of the costs and benefits of such activities as entail the deficits. This is a specific example of the statement made earlier in this chapter about the influence of the national debt on distribution of income. To an indefinite extent wartime profiteers pay back some of their profits in postwar taxes which are used to pay interest to bondholders. On the other hand, postwar changes in price or interest levels may hurt or help bondholders. Similarly, postwar price changes may heighten or reduce the real value of war profits.

Even short of the crisis of war or acute depression, considerations of this sort may have a bearing on the handling of public budgets. The public has many interests, not single interests to be served by some single slogan. Bondholders, as one economist remarks, are not a race of people who do not own stocks. Bondholders, salary and wage receivers, all alike might depend for their very existence on a slowly rising price level and a budgetary deficit. The proper test of budgetary practice is in an expanding economy and improved general welfare, not in the mystical term "balancing."

The related "pay-as-you-go" phrase is uttered most often with reference to state and local government, where it has some greater applicability than it does to national governmental finance. Yet the phrase reflects a do-nothing attitude hostile to both progress and thoughtfulness. State and local governments must manage their activities, and must put the meeting of their responsibilities for action above any dictum. Good management will entail borrowing on occasion, and carrying a more or less continuing debt. Even though they do not have and cannot have the fundamental resources and facilities appropriate to the national level of government, they do have a certain basic importance and some special resources. Notably, they have the long life expectancy which makes their forward fiscal problems, as seen today, less serious when they actually emerge in later decades.

Legislators at all levels of government are thoroughly aware of the widespread belief that budgetary deficits are evil, and they do not lightly affront such deeply held convictions. Congress, especially, is well aware of the fact that fiscal prejudice is particularly pointed toward limiting action by the national government. But Congress in many instances clearly prefers a comparatively small deficit to a tax increase. It prefers to hope that receipts will increase without a higher tax rate. It clearly prefers a somewhat obfuscated distribution of monetary costs involved in meeting crises. It prefers, similarly, a somewhat obscure and very complicated economic situation in which people try various ways to advance their interests and cannot be too certain how far, or whether, or in just what way they have bettered themselves. This is, after all, not an all-planned, all-directed economy but is a capitalist economic system in which ingenuity in pursuit of advantage is normal, and loss not unusual. It is also a democratic governmental system in which elected officials would be overwhelmed if all citizens could hold them quite precisely responsible for every aspect of their condition.

Congress acts accordingly, and the economists, critically observing what transpires, are coming in quite large numbers to regard the record with almost as much awe as shock. One writes in a personal letter, "It seems to me that government expenditures for social overhead might be permitted to cause a deficit even in prosperity, if new developments are being undertaken." He adds, "This is the great problem of underdeveloped areas; there is always threat of inflation, but without the inflationary threat the economy is doomed to stagnation." So we come directly to the phenomenon of inflation.

Inflation

At the present stage of civilization the insistence upon rigid budget balancing is either a lingering echo of a more primitive time, or it is designed to oppose some kinds of governmental action. In the same way, the appearance of panic some persons whip themselves into over "the threat of inflation" or "our shrinking dollar" is either parrot-patter or a way of drumming up opposition to some competitive interest. Debt, budget balancing, and inflation are obviously three aspects of the same set of intertwined phenomena, and much that needs to be said about inflation has already been said.

There are many sides to the price phenomenon. The buggy business was not the victim of inflation; fashions, obsolescence, invention, the saving provided by an improved technology—these and many other things can cause prices of particular commodities to rise or fall. The fruits of improved production may be concentrated, or divided between price reductions, wage increases, and profits. Wage increases may be partially absorbed or wholly passed to consumers in the form of increased prices. A speculative orgy in one kind of property or another may greatly increase prices of such property.

The point is simply that inflation may be privately induced or aggravated, or governmentally induced or aggravated, but that in any case any vital economy must provide some room for price adjustments to changed competitive, usage, and technological conditions. Whether or not a particular price change is inflationary in character often can be ascertained only through special analysis. Neither a particular demand for increased wages nor a particular commodity price increase is inevitably inflationary.

Inflation may be of at least four possible orders. The first of these is exemplified by the long-term depreciation of the Portuguese *reis* which in the course of centuries gave way to the *milreis* —originally worth a thousand *reis*. This is a rather strictly monetary phenomenon, developing either fitfully or fairly steadily, but taking on a dramatic character only when considered in very long-time terms.

The second order of inflation is at the opposite end of the time scale—galloping or runaway inflation. This kind of inflation was experienced in the Confederacy at the time of our Civil War, in Germany after World War I, and later in China. It is associated with war, revolution, and general economic and political ruin.

A third variety of inflation is the seesaw or cyclical type. It may represent a kind of spontaneous or semidirected phenomenon of economic adjustment, but, if left to itself, it is capable of overcompensating and making more trouble than it has relieved.

A fourth variety of inflation is to be found in a fairly moderate, irregularly continuous, and rather tightly directed rise in prices.

While the components of statistics vary so much in significance over a long period of time that comparisons of successive periods for a century or more have only a rough and illustrative validity, the United States, apart from the Confederacy, may be said to have had, in the course of its history, inflation of the third and fourth kinds, with war being the major factor in both cases. In such terms as it is possible to deduce, the price level has risen here from about 70 in 1770 to about 270 in 1956. It was at about 220 during the Revolutionary War, about 90 afterwards; at about 185 at the time of the War of 1812, 97 thereafter; at about 195 at the time of the Civil War, dropping rather steadily for 25 years thereafter to about 65; rising slowly thereafter and then sharply to the World War I peak of about 215; dropping again to 100 in 1930; and then rising fairly steadily since then to about 270 in 1956.

The remarkable fact is that there was no significant drop after World War II or after the Korean activity. If we leave out the rise and fall associated with World War I, the American price level has risen fairly steadily since about 1894, from a low of 65 to a high of 270. Almost precisely 115 of these points are attrib-

utable either to World War I or to World War II, and perhaps
90 points to the general phenomenon of price increase. This
general increase amounts to about 1.45 points a year on the
average.

It is difficult to translate the points just cited into meaningful
percentages because of the war factors. However, if it is understood that the two sets of figures are two different ways of seeing
the price-change phenomenon, it may be helpful to cite some
figures developed by the First National City Bank of New York.
The bank had sought from all important governments information about price changes, and received reports from thirty-five.
These showed the value of money in terms of cost of living or
consumer price formulations for the ten-year period 1948-58.
Ranked according to the *least* depreciation of currencies, the first
ten nations were, in order: Portugal, Switzerland, Belgium, Ecuador, Germany, India, United States, Venezuela, Pakistan, and
Canada.

This indicates that, among the thirty-five reporting nations,
the United States ranks seventh in price-level stability. The data
indicate at the same time that for a ten-year postwar period the
price level rose on a compounded basis 1.8 per cent a year. The
comparable average annual price change in Canada was 2.5 per
cent, almost one and a half times as fast. Yet Canada has been
experiencing a period of high prosperity and is surely not in any
visible danger of a runaway inflation.

In his widely used economics text, referred to earlier in this
chapter, Paul Samuelson says, "If price inflation could be held
down to, say, 2 per cent per year, such a mild steady inflation
need not cause too great alarm." I agree, and believe further that
a small amount of inflation rather steadily maintained will make
the economy more manageable and more certainly advancing
than a thoroughly stable price level would. My own preference,
however, would be for a normal target percentage of 1¼ per cent
to 1¾ per cent, leaving somewhat greater changes to be made
when there is special need or special opportunity. After we have
had longer peacetime periods of experience with these matters,
better guides can be formulated.

Private actions can upset guides and efforts of the kind just suggested. In the absence of some fair and sensible guidelines some employee groups may push for too frequent and too large pay and benefits increases. More frequently, violence is likely to be done to the kind of economic order here espoused through the extension of administered pricing by some of the key and potent industries, with the effect of capturing for these economic power groups a larger share of the national income.

This kind of thing could lead to a distortion of the economy and to a major political crisis. The alternative is an assumption of more responsibility by citizens. This requires some new social learning which would sublimate conflicts of interest and produce new efforts at common betterment through improved production and substantial expansion of public services.

In any case, the strivings for betterment by labor and by management, whether excessively competitive or reasonably cooperative, are implicit in and stimulated by economic capitalism and political democracy, not particularly by fiscal policy of government. Indeed, it seems to me increasingly clear as we gain experience with these two novel and developing social forms that *both political democracy and highly developed capitalism are facilitated by fairly continuous but variable and restrained inflation and deficit financing, with consequential debt increments.*

Inflation *seems* inevitably to profit government at all levels when it does not proceed too rapidly. It profits government in the sense that governmental debt of any given amount diminishes in monetary significance in the course of time. The gain in this is actually the taxpayers', since inflation reduces—as a proportion of all income—the amount of taxes that must be raised to meet debt interest. This therefore frees resources that government budget-makers can devote to other purposes without affecting taxes.

During the long life of which government is capable, prior developed public debt and prior tax rates become relatively smaller also when considered in terms of the enlarged economy. Tax resource potentialities become expanded because of the increase in total real worth and income.

Altogether, citizens have tended to worry too much about the debt, the budget, and inflation. This is not to say that able

management of public finance is not required; it is to insist that
we approach the future in an economic position that should be
confidence inspiring. Good management, imagination, ingenuity,
invention, and time will make the dimensions of the feasible very
much greater than the dull and fearful are ready to believe.

Taxation Patterns

The political aversion to tax levies is so strong that it may
be regarded as almost axiomatic that in any decently structured
political jurisdiction of democratic character any governmentally
approved tax increase is much needed. It is not equally certain
that its incidence will be appropriately and equitably designed.
Local property assessments, for example, almost invariably put
proportionately higher tax costs on the shoulders of renters and
those householders who own small and cheap houses than on
those who occupy large and costly establishments. At the state
and national levels, powerful interests are especially likely to
secure special favors through key legislators because the complexity of the matters involved tends to obscure the results.

Taxation according to ability to pay and its corollary principle
of progressivity make acceptable general guides, but the taxes
available to the different governmental jurisdictions make them
hard, and in some respects impossible, to apply. Various features
of different taxes in a single jurisdiction or level of government
so interact as to make the results difficult to appraise. The interaction of the various taxes levied by different levels of government is a further complication. (A substantial part of any state
income tax increase, for example, is derived, in effect, from the
United States Government, since the increased state payment is a
deductible item on national income tax returns.)

A second basic consideration is the fact that the tax pattern,
private and public subsidies, salaries and wages are economic
elements affecting incentive and economic expansion. While
modern society has learned that a successful economy does not
require a range in incentive extending from starvation to an
annual income of scores of millions, the question of how much
inducement should be offered, and to whom, has not been very
thoroughly explored.

We do know that the incentive needed varies according to time and place, persons and situations. In Britain during World War II, for example, the agricultural authorities would assign to the management of a competent farmer a tract removed from the control of its owner because it was not well farmed. The man given the new responsibility, requiring harder work, could not net as much as sixpence more than before, because of a 100 per cent excess-profits tax. The incentive of national survival made an economic incentive unnecessary.

A remark of the late Jay Hormel, then head of the Hormel Packing Company, one noontime about 1940, provides a different example. Sitting on an upstairs porch overlooking his landscaped acres in a small Minnesota city, he spoke thoughtfully to this point: "I can spend only about a third of my income. I can spend that much only by spending a good deal through agents, and one doesn't get much feeling of spending by doing it that way. *If I had been born at a time* when I could have earned only 10 per cent of what I now earn, I'd have worked just as hard. But don't think I'd let anybody take any of this away from me now."

Systematic annual tabulations of the actual results of existing tax laws on incomes in successive brackets above one hundred thousand dollars should be made readily available to press and public through a suitably competent and reputable medium such as the Council of Economic Advisors, or the House Committee on Government Operations. Such tabulations should be in varied terms, showing how much of the income in each bracket was of the long-term capital gain sort, showing sizes of gifts on which taxes were paid, showing dimensions of trusts established, etc. Such information would permit economists and politicians to stimulate appropriate public discussion.

There is no doubt now that there is a vast amount of difference in taxes paid on large incomes of approximately the same size, and that a tightening of the general pattern could result in a very substantial drop in the theoretical top brackets. There is similarly no doubt that the public and the Congress should pay more attention to the capital gains tax, around which a whole new economy has developed, and to the depletion allowances for incomes derived from gas and oil.

The principal concern of citizens should be to find ways in which secrecy for individual taxpayers—which itself is not sacrosanct—may not result in too much general ignorance about the tax realities. While taxation is in many ways a highly technical matter, it is possible to depict its consequences intelligibly, and on the general character of the tax patterns public judgment can have a peculiar competence.

A valuable and succinct summary of the incidence of taxes was issued in May, 1960, by the Tax Foundation, a research organization financed and directed by leaders in American economic affairs. Such a source guarantees as much authenticity as the available data permit. This Tax Foundation study shows that there is for the American tax system as a whole practically no "progressivity" up to the bracket of taxpayers whose incomes surpass $15,000, and much less than is generally believed in brackets above $15,000. Actually, insofar as such a fine distinction is valid under the limitations of available data, families with incomes under $2,000 pay in all kinds of taxes, directly and indirectly, a higher percentage of their incomes than the average for all taxpayers. Leaving out social security taxes, the percentage of income going to taxes is almost exactly the same for all brackets up to $15,000.

This situation is primarily a result of the character of state and local taxes. In state and local taxes, families with less than $2,000 incomes pay a higher proportion of their incomes than the average in all other income brackets. In state and local taxes the smallest percentage of total income is paid by families in the highest income brackets.

Great need exists for more studies of this sort, and for political discussion concentrated on them. The tax *pattern* is far more important to most citizens than a balanced budget, the size of the national debt, or the rate of any inflation we are likely to experience.

XII

The General Welfare

MUCH MORE widely here than in any other advanced country, the phrase "welfare state" is used in lieu of reflection as a way of prejudging policy. It seems to be assumed that the idea of welfare being furthered through the instrumentality of government is a new and radical one.

Actually, the use of government to enhance the general welfare is as old as government, as old as social order. Early meanings of "commonweal" were "a commonwealth," and "the general welfare." Definitions of "commonwealth," in turn, are "the people of a state," "a state in which the people rule," "a republic," and, latterly, "a body of persons united by some common interest and viewed as equals in authority." It is also, by statute, the official title of four of our states—Kentucky, Massachusetts, Pennsylvania, and Virginia. The root term from which these words are derived, "weal," means "welfare," and all of them tie strongly to considerations of mutual interest and to governmental instrumentalities.

Governments exist because their adherents believe they offer more general welfare than any visible and attainable alternative. An institution that maintains internal order, defends against attack from outside, manages a satisfactory monetary system, keeps records of and upholds property rights, serves and oversees a mutual enrichment through trade, provides fire protection, disease quarantines, and sanitation standards—any such institution is a welfare instrument. These are, of course, not the only means by which welfare is secured and enhanced, but such governmental activities are essential, and are, indeed, the only way in which the welfare of everybody may be made a fairly consistent focus of concern. How successfully this concern may be served depends upon the structures of government, the qualities of leadership and followership within it, the extent of popular knowledge and expectations at a particular time, and the availability of financial resources. The ancient "poor farm," for example, gives way to something better as we learn what is better and increase in capacity to do better.

Every active phase of life is a pursuit of well-being as seen, organized, and directed by some persons or groups, or by people generally. The primary danger is that less than the whole public good will be sought, meaning that some special private concern will dominate. At the other extreme, there is danger that the general public will not respect foresight and breadth of concern but instead will impose shortsightedness and mediocrity.

Even though perhaps veering at times toward one or the other of these dangers, the advance of civilization is an effort to enlarge the scope of welfare. The private effort may be, as with us, to invent and produce new things, to make more things, to do more things, to enlarge knowledge, understanding, and the facilities favorable to personal achievement. It may improve technologies, open new and richer storehouses of natural resources, build homes, communities, and urban conglomerates. It may provide personal mobility and works of art but complicate and confuse personal and social affairs. In contrast it may open opportunities for exploitation and the attainment of domineering status. In any case, the basic orientation of all private efforts is and must be toward the rather readily visible, close-up concerns of self-interest.

The public efforts of mankind are similarly rooted in self-interest but differ in capacity for foresight, broader vision, and the service of interpersonal and social equities. Under democratic government, while responsibility for specific achievements in pursuit of the general welfare rests in leadership, responsibility for the general character of the work of leaders rests with the citizens who choose leaders and make demands upon them. If citizen exactions from public leadership merely reflect the most vivid private concerns, even those will not be well served.

Small private advances in civilization can be sustained only if there are complementary advances in the public field. Private and public welfare pursuits reinforce each other. The availability of large resources, broad scope, and long-life expectancy make government peculiarly capable of carrying general responsibility. Popular control makes this responsibility inescapable. People tend to try to do those things for which they are especially responsible, and to serve those to whom they are accountable. Only officials have the necessary access to resources, and only officials are especially responsible for particular actions, decisions, policies, and programs promoting the general welfare. In democracy, citizens as sovereigns are obliged to try to overcome the limitations of their private vantage points and to attain a shared concern for general equity and fair dealing.

The greatest change the world has ever seen has been the enormous acceleration during recent decades in the rate and scope of change itself. This seems to be a consequence of a kind of feedback transfer of dynamic energy from the private to the public field in the case of particular developments. The invention of the "horseless carriage" has been cited earlier to illustrate the way in which private activity imposes new responsibility on government. It seems similarly to involve a feedback of energy from government to the private scene in the case of general developments such as the extension of public education and governmental sponsorship of basic research. The democratic idea itself has general influence in shaping demands of citizens, such as those made for newly feasible approaches to equality of opportunity for the young.

In any case, the main distinction seems to hold that public welfare effort in this country is oriented to the general social condition, private welfare effort to self and nearest colleagues. Both are pursuits of real values. The father who devotes his energies to idealistic soapbox oratory and fails to support his family is not a good citizen, but neither is the one who limits his social responsibility to being a "good provider." History has made it abundantly clear that personal welfare and general welfare are mutually dependent and must progress together. To express opposition to the welfare state is equivalent to opposing civilization.

Prejudices to Challenge

Hostility to welfare achieved through government derives from a general hostility toward government especially widespread in the United States. It results also from a natural preoccupation with private interests, which here have their greatest magnitude and variety, and from a resultant mental exaggeration of the actual scope and capacity of private enterprise.

In the chapter entitled "Life in a Free Society," attention is given to some of the limitations inherent in private enterprise. While many private enterprises make important and essential contributions to our well-being, not any or all of them would seek or accept responsibility for the general welfare. Indeed, private enterprise can flourish here to our advantage only because government can and does take care of many consequences of business which are not merely beyond the ken of private enterprise but often entirely outside its competence. The new automobile business made employment in the buggy business obsolete, for example, but naturally assumed no responsibility for the particular workers who were displaced. The new industry sold cars to many buyers only because government kept providing traffic arrangements and highways.

Exaggeration of the scope and sufficiency of private enterprise is a remnant of the old laissez-faire notion that when everyone pursues his selfish interest zealously and single-mindedly, the general interest will be served automatically. From the beginning of time, and increasingly with the advance of civilization, society's demands for governmental action have belied this thoughtless generalization.

There is another related attitude, still vigorous, still revered, and notably hypocritical, since it is often expressed by some who are most generously subsidized: "Subsidies are inherently evil." This is often said by stockholders in air transport companies and ocean shipping companies, by industrialists whose products are bulwarked by protective tariffs, by cattlemen with vested interests in the public domain, by attorneys for these interests, by persons who inherited wealth, and by many others more than ordinarily favored by government, family, society, or circumstance. The position really seems to be that "subsidies are wrong for everybody but me and possibly some of my associates."

All of the subsidies mentioned, including some of those usually attributed to "circumstance," have been bestowed by government. The social and economic orders in which inheritances are accumulated are products of governance. The right to transmit wealth by gift and bequest is provided by statutory enactments and the administration of law, and the specific transmitting mechanisms of trust funds, gift provisos, and capital gains tax limits facilitate perpetuation of privilege. All of these arrangements are made by government, presumably because they are thought to contribute to the general welfare.

There would be little popular disposition to say that these subsidies weaken the beneficiaries. Most people do not really believe that when the recipients of subsidies are privileged folk the result of the subsidies is debilitating, demoralizing, or evil. The argument against subsidies often seems designed to keep the underprivileged in an underprivileged condition and to support the belief that bestowing privileges upon the privileged makes a welfare program sound.

This line of examination has brought us close to the most sweeping of this particular family of prejudices: "Everyone must himself earn whatever he gets." A third of a century ago one of the law partners of Senator Albert B. Cummins used to assert that under laissez-faire everyone, without exception, would earn everything he got, no more, no less, however he got it. The point was that it is unwise and useless to try to help anyone, especially those most in need. It is true, of course, that aid can be unwisely given. But it is also true that privileges are usually advantages and that often when persons of privilege prove inadequate it is for lack of something else—possibly insufficient parental attention, the absence of a sense of function and responsibility, or some similar disadvantage.

The idea that anyone can earn everything he receives is, of course, nonsense. The baby does not and can never earn the milk he receives from his mother, or the parental affection and care that surround him. He cannot earn the civilization into which he is born, the books available for him to read, the structures, experience, and other achievements of bygone generations which are his free inheritance. That these boons are not to be paid for does not ruin the individual or the society. If debilitation were the usual product of unearned advantage, the pursuit of savagery would be as sensible as the pursuit of civilization.

Life is always difficult enough, and many more persons are overwhelmed by underprivilege than by privilege. Still more are handicapped, and fall short of their potential achievements, because of their diversion of too many energies into earning things that come to others unearned. There is difficulty enough in supplying all the tempering, all the disciplining, all the drive and sensibility one may need. A higher level of welfare simply reveals new challenges and new difficulties, as a new scientific insight raises questions not thought of earlier. There is no need, then, to enforce hardship or to manufacture difficulties.

Help Is Often Helpful

That advantages generally are benefits, not handicaps, is usually understood by persons in terms of themselves, but not so often recognized in terms of others and in relationship to social development as a whole. The blind prejudice against welfare as a governmental objective has discouraged the achievement of skills and the understanding of established practices.

Provision for receiverships, or for personal and corporate bankruptcy, and the use of income, status, and security incentives, including the use of subsidies, are elementary features of our whole social order, and are of very ancient origin. The more dynamic is a society, the more forms do these devices take; the more advanced is a society, the larger are the resources of wealth and learning that are available to put to work to make further increases in resources.

No private enterprise or association of enterprises can underwrite general welfare, but within themselves they can and do use welfare techniques increasingly as forms of "good administration." The very employment of anyone in modern business usually entails an initial loss on the part of the employer. In other words, the employee is subsidized. It costs money to induct and train employees. With increasing frequency additional costs take the form of later subsidies, including the financing of graduate study. These techniques are no less useful in their broader and more diverse applications through the agency of government.

To provide incentive proportionate to the kind and degree of competence needed is to encourage, to impart motivation, to advise, supervise, and to educate. This help takes such form as guidance to individual owners of filling stations by the great oil companies. Automobile manufacturers similarly advise garage owners on size of car and parts inventories, repair charges, accounting methods, and management in general. Advice also is given by home-office specialists to managers of individual units in chain store systems; thus many who have proved unable to survive in their own businesses are enabled to serve as highly successful managers. The costs involved in such methods are offset by a reduction in the rate of employee turnover, similar reductions in customer turnover, and by a decrease in small-enterprise failures.

Social workers engaged in governmental programs and the field staff of such agencies as the Farmers' Home Administration similarly reduce social waste and similarly associate financial assistance with "supervision" and guidance, often feeling that the guidance is more important than the money even though it would usually be useless without the money. The regrettable thing is that so little of the significant experience in these programs has been made available to the public in readable form.

I have visited hundreds of beneficiaries of some of these newer and more personal forms of governmental welfare activity here and in other countries, and have been greatly moved and impressed by their progress and their responsible attitudes. Illustratively, I cite the single case of a southern farmer who had borrowed three hundred dollars from the Farmers' Home Administration's predecessor agency. The agency's county supervisor and I were driving down a country road when my companion spied this particular farmer walking a short way ahead. He slowed his car, saying, "I want to talk with this man; he impressed me favorably, but he turned sour as soon as we made him the loan." As we stopped beside the farmer he turned, recognized the official, and with lighted face spoke eagerly: "I'm so glad to see you. Ever since I borrowed that money I've been almost sick; I couldn't see how I could ever pay back three hundred dollars, but now I think I can begin to see my way to do it—it's going to work out, and I wanted you to know." He had "turned sour" because he took his responsibility seriously. He paid his loan in due course.

Governmental aid of so personal a sort is pitched in terms of large areas of need on the part of many persons. Programs are designed and adopted as general, not special, aids. Some of these things obviously are more feasible for government than for any other institutions; some of the more important ones simply carry the conventional service of insurance to the dimension of social insurance against catastrophe. Some, like the U.S. Employment Offices and the public schools, simply provide a service.

Aid, then, is commonly extended by private practice and by public action, in mutual interest. From infancy on through old age we get benefits we have not earned and, through hard work, tax payments, business practice, benevolence and good will we somewhat absentmindedly make our individual contributions to society.

A Few Things Learned

On the negative side it should be recognized that a gift or even a loan in dimensions wholly beyond the bounds of the recipient's past ability to manage has little chance of being useful and may be distinctly hurtful. The loan of $300 to the farmer who had then "turned sour" was tailored almost precisely as it should have been. Perhaps it would have been more certainly effective if fixed at $275, but some things requiring money needed to be done, and a plan of action less than adequate certainly would not have sufficed. There was need also to encourage the borrower to stretch his abilities to about the maximum point where he would feel equal to his responsibility. Such considerations are central to really helpful action. There is an analogy between a gift or a loan too big and a fortune earned too quickly. Some of our oil millionaires illustrate the point vividly, but they have comrades in immaturity among others of the so-called self-made men. Further on the negative side, it is to be recognized that aid efforts need to be timed. Two hundred years ago a proposal to require all children to attend school until they were sixteen years old would have been absurdly inappropriate and unpersuasive. Available resources would not have permitted it, and the need for schooling had not reached that point. Indeed, we have not yet shaped curricula, teaching materials, and teacher equipment in ways fully appropriate to the requirements.

New welfare programs can be most wisely introduced, then, when they appear to be the logical next step, when beneficiaries will quickly utilize them as a matter of right rather than as a product of benevolence, and when the aid given helps to round out personal resources of the recipients by achieving *a better balance in their advantages.* Contributions by prospective beneficiaries are desirable where feasible, supporting the conviction that benefits come as a matter of right. It is especially important to give preference to programs that validly enhance the individual sense of being socially useful and recognized.

Welfare efforts that are sanctimonious or condescending, with pretensions to unadulterated generosity, are likely to be as phony and as ineffective as claims to social value resting only on rate of profit or salary "earned." A shell game is still a shell game, even if it is conducted on Madison Avenue. The sound pursuit of welfare is based on a recognition of mutual dependence and carried on as a common effort, with sympathy, sensitiveness, integrity, and practicality.

International Welfare, Too

All of these learnings apply to the enlarged community in which we now are so inextricably involved. The peoples of the world have become thoroughly interdependent. As the richest nation in the world we are the one most jealously regarded, the one with most to lose from world frustration and disorder, the one with most to gain from an improved sense of well-being on the part of our neighbors.

Carlyle wrote about the family of privilege located high on a mountainside above a squalid city, stubbornly refusing to be concerned about lack of sanitation arrangements in the city. When the plague came, wrote Carlyle, it did not stop at the foot of the mountain. So with us, working together in a common cause with peoples in underdeveloped nations is the only possible way to our future well-being, and to avoidance of incipient plague.

At best, of course, we can only co-operate. We should not, therefore, exaggerate the cost to us as we did, for example, during World War II, when many Americans thought we were the principal source of the food eaten by our allies. Altogether the food shipped from the United States at the height of the war represented just about 10 per cent of all the food moving on the seven seas, and ocean shipments constituted an extremely small portion of the total food supply.

Lend-lease food shipments amounted to less than our increases in food production during the war years, so that the American people actually had more to eat during the war than before the war. Beef did not figure in the lend-lease program, and the "beef shortage" of which so many complained was wholly a product of military consumption and increased civilian demand. The increased food consumption of men in the services was equivalent to an increase of four million in population. Increase in employment, increase in wages, and diversion of buying power from things like automobiles, not available during the war, were far more responsible for our sense of food shortage than were our shipments to allies.

The common cause was vividly apparent in wartime, and therefore there was not much feeling that we were being generous, as, of course, we were not. We were merely co-operating in a common, desperate business. The international aid program of recent years should be similarly regarded. There is little likelihood that we shall become so very enlightened that we will do as much as we should; there is no danger at all that we will do too much. There is always danger that we may not act wisely enough. But our greatest concern should be to make it clear beyond any doubt that we recognize our part in a common responsibility.

The task is to help improve economic output in terms so large and so continuing that benevolence alone would be inadequate. What we can do, even with our relatively great wealth, will be much less than will be needed: we are, after all, less than 7 per cent of the world's population. But we certainly can and must help, and we have by now enough experience in the international field so that some of our leadership is beginning to learn how to carry on this kind of co-operation.

There are four erroneous popular attitudes about foreign aid which lead Congress to take mistaken positions concerning it. First of all, as in the case of food supplies provided our allies in wartime, the public greatly exaggerates the number of persons engaged in foreign assistance and its monetary cost in proportion to the total outlays being made. Secondly, the aid appropriations are made for too short periods, thus greatly handicapping the recipient nations in both planning and operations. The appropriations should be made for at least five-year terms. Thirdly, the appropriations are tied too rigidly to the provision of "technical assistance," the need for which is generally exaggerated and in any case not uniform among underdeveloped nations. The greatest and most uniform need is for dollar exchange. Finally, any requirements for expending the dollar aid in the United States, in the first instance, put an undue hardship on the recipient nations and are unrewarding to us. Dollar aid is as valuable as it is because it *ultimately* can and will be spent only in the American market in any case.

Internationally and domestically, welfare programs involve a mild redistribution of buying power associated with concerted efforts designed to increase productive capacity and political order. The ends sought are of general advantage. Business leaders experienced in the development of mass markets are increasingly vigorous proponents of welfare efforts. A citizenry proud of a national capacity for "thinking big" will not fail to see an expansion of well-being as the continuing objective essential to its own further enrichment.

XIII

Relying on Evolution

IN PRECEDING pages, citizens have been urged to
engage in party activities in a systematic way in their local units.
Most of them will not find this easy to do. They will find no open
door, no warm welcome, perhaps no welcome at all. This will
seem surprising, in view of the fundamental need of parties to
secure adherents. Yet it should not be as surprising as it usually
is. Even in an evangelical church one does not readily get a
chance at much more than "busywork."

Volunteer workers are everywhere considered by professionals
to be possible sources of trouble. Dollar-a-year men are not prized
by career politicians or by civil servants, and generally are not
very effective in governmental posts. Acceptable organizational
activity requires a discipline which is associated most commonly
with an important source of income. It is associated also with
experience. Professional political leaders at all levels have had
many unhappy experiences with zealous neophytes who expect
to come to influence too quickly, who speak out of turn and without realizing their lack of background or their limitations as
recruits. The newcomers may not know what to treat as confi-
dential, or lack either inclination or capacity to keep it so. They
are likely to lack organizational understanding and skill.

To say that none of these objections applies to a particular person who seeks to be accepted as a recruit is not enough; the party professionals must be convinced of this, and only sustained action—not verbal protestations—convince. The professionals have a case, too. For all their closed-shop attitude, they are the ones who survive. It is somewhat typical that only a few years after Clark and Dilworth took over Philadelphia in a competent, dedicated, and badly needed reform effort, rather conventional party organizations edged into much of their old dominance.

This is significant, and it is even more so that aside from Joseph S. Clark, Jr. and Richardson Dilworth, the populous and important state of Pennsylvania since the days of Franklin has not produced a single even second-rank political figure whom one may identify without research. Up to now, for the most part in most places most of the time, the persons who could and did work steadily at party business have been pretty limited fellows. Still, they have worked at it, and they have learned moderately well how to get support with the general voter situation as it is. They have their limitations. But citizens who wish to participate in bettering the quality of political efforts will have to learn things equivalent to what the pros know, and act with similar effectiveness. It will be slow work.

The same things apply in a way to the problems of reform and improvement of the formal organs of government. There are no effective wands for political tourists to wave that will bring our dreams to realization. So intelligent, able, and dedicated a man as Averell Harriman, experienced as he was in appointive governmental posts, became a candidate for elective office first at the age of sixty-three, and then at the level of governor of New York. Certainly if he had had terms in the state legislature and other minor elective offices for fifteen or twenty years he would have had a brilliant record in the upper reaches of politics. No one should seek a governorship, much less the Presidency, without long, prior *political* experience.

The most devoted and responsible patriot may in time of severe crisis or great opportunity turn his efforts toward establishment of an enlarged political entity in which his own country is to be in some measure submerged. In such a time did Winston Churchill offer union to invaded and collapsing France.

Learning in the crisis of World War II resulted in establishment of the Common Market among six nations of Western Europe, stimulating the most rapid recent increase in economic well-being the world has seen, and thereby attracting other members. It is also, by intention of some of its leaders at least, a substantial step toward a United States of Europe.

With insight born of necessity, and with extended application of the aspirations of their own peoples, Britain and France have been abandoning imperial control of colonies, encouraging free affiliation where that is desired and permitting full separation elsewhere.

The survival of treasured values thus is assured by breadth, generosity, imagination, and enlightenment in achieving political transformation. This is sublimation of nationalism, not treason. It is an expression of strength in avoiding catastrophe and in meeting successfully the buffetings of time and change.

In much the same way, the United States came into being when, with the Confederation failing, an unsurpassed group of contemporary statesmen went beyond their assignment to produce a wholly new Constitution and a nation in fact.

As a usual thing, however, historical crises have had no logical and dependable aftermaths. The ending of an eruption has seen no establishment of adequate instruments with which to pursue the objectives of those whose needs and aspirations were dramatized in the crisis. During and just following the disorder and confusion usually attendant upon crisis, there have been few important political inventions successfully fulfilling the hopes of those who ignited the fuse of explosion. The United States is one of the rare cases where there has been a rather unbroken subsequent pursuit and unfolding of the values sought in the War of Independence. The more common pattern is revolution and counterrevolution, sometimes in serial installments.

The familiar story of France is extreme, but illustrative. The fall of the French monarchy in successive steps beginning in 1789 was followed in 1792 by the First Republic, in 1795 by The Directory, in 1799 by the Consulate of Napoleon, which gave way to the First Empire in 1804, the restoration of the Bourbons in 1815, the revolution of 1830 and the vesting of power then in

Louis Philippe. The revolution of 1848 established the Second Republic, taken over and converted into the Third Empire by Louis Napoleon in 1851, since when there have been the Third, Fourth, and Fifth Republics, with many incidental constitutional crises.

In other words, crisis is extremely risky, its impromptu and drastic adjustments unlikely to serve the long-run needs. Yet crisis is foreshadowed whenever social changes of internal or external sort accumulate, wherever serious discrimination and injustice are long continued, wherever political and social adjustments are incommensurate with the heightened strains and complications of governance. Confidence in the future can be strong only as we demonstrate ability to make continuing and frequent adjustments that enable us to avoid acute crisis.

The Drift toward Crisis

Never before now in the course of history has there been so much change in the world—never so extensive, never so complicated, and never at such a pace as in recent decades. Technology, the advance of learning, the shrinking world, and the awakened aspiration of the millions in countries less developed and less fortunate than ours distinguish this period. The outside stresses give more force and meaning to our need for compassion and decency toward the patient Negro. Concern for survival of our civilization is heavily involved in this domestic problem, and makes dangerous as well as stupid such practices as the display of Confederate flags in national political conventions and other assemblages. Yet this is only one area in which we are out of adjustment with our times. The very multitude of changes in a short period makes our way an extreme deviation from the ancient course of history carried on generally through settled and repetitious ways.

The thinking and the ingenuity that have gone into the acceleration of latter-day change are not directed at the general order but at specific things. Just so were the inventors of the "horseless carriage" disregardful of what they were doing to and for people, industries, and government. The call for cement and steel for road construction, the consumer demand for rubber tires, the

need for the restrictions of traffic lights, as well as the development of park systems and a great recreation industry have
changed the face of the country and the manner of life. They
have also added greatly to the responsibilities of government.
Countless other developments have been under way concurrently.

The multitude of specific changes requires general adjustments,
largely in political and governmental terms, for only these are
responsible for the general ordering of the fruits of many private
activities domestically, and for relating our country to a world
in which adjustments of similar and yet different sorts are potentially explosive in crisis. Survival of Western civilization
depends upon its capacity to make such general adjustments as
have been effected through the great genius of the British people,
who constitute now the oldest continuing political order in the
world. Avoidance of crisis will require not only co-operation
with such peoples, but development of our own powers of adjustment and readiness to make use of them. Avoidance of crisis is
by no means confined to managing the competitive threat of
Communist powers.

We may be too much preoccupied with the business of weaving
our way through the traffic of civilization to attend to civilization
itself. We seem too much disposed to espouse doctrines of prim-
itivists such as Mills, Whyte, and Boulding, who suffer acute
forms of Parkinson's disorganizational disease, rather than to
turn our attention to insuring the life of the social order.

Scientists are fond of reminding us that each advance in learning, while answering some earlier question, reveals new questions
which pose new problems. This is also true of social advance.
Every attainment complicates and enlarges social problems, calling for further development of social capacity.

Achievements in the field of health increase population, putting
new demands on food supply, education, and housing facilities.
They increase the proportion of the aged, who are more likely
than younger citizens to be tied to views and practices becoming
obsolescent and so disposed to hamper governmental adjustments. Old folk also require pensions and special care.

Technology is changing and has changed the nature of farming
and farm life at a fast pace. The economy as a whole in this

country has reached the place where it is no longer merely something to maintain and to pyramid. It bears little resemblance to the economy of 1900, and still less to that of 1870. Our new emphasis on economic expansion through "want-creation" is pointed sharply toward trivia, duplication of effort, waste, doodads, and phony values. This slant deprives much employment of dignity, and impairs integrity. The corruption of one division of the Food and Drug Administration, disclosed early in 1960, as well as fraud in the quiz shows and "payola" reflect unprincipled business enterprises and unprincipled advertising agencies. In many areas where outright corruption has not been disclosed there has been a glorification of corruption's stepbrother, vulgarity.

These things are for the most part not to be handled by government, but they are nonetheless a part of the responsibility of citizens who can set the tone of a society. And these phenomena are one expression of a society confused, losing its sense of direction and responsibility. The tempo and dimensions of changes in manifold features of our life strain basic social arrangements designed for much simpler and much more slowly changing conditions.

Problems of all kinds have come to involve steadily more considerations, and most problems are of an increasingly technical character. Even though scarcity and subsistence problems are disappearing in our economy, private concerns are becoming more demanding for reasons similar to those making public problems difficult and crucial. The resulting tendency to give almost exclusive preference to private and personal concerns in the face of modern interdependence makes us unaware of our public inadequacies.

Our eminence in the world has come principally on account of our great wealth, based on natural resources preserved here during long ages before our forebears came, and quickly subject to the most stupendous exploitation because of the concurrence of our beginnings and the beginnings of modern science and technology. Our world eminence, in other words, has been earned primarily within the United States, and yet world eminence has little meaning and can offer us little security except as it is *exercised* outside our boundaries. Our internal achievements do not particularly fit us for the necessary external performance.

These are some of the elements that, without relevant social adjustments, contribute to a drift toward crisis.

There are conscientious citizens who sense the drift or some features of it. There are those who feel that all would be well if only we would disarm, or secure a disarmament compact with the Soviet bloc. Yet disarmament would be futile, wasteful, and highly dangerous apart from some more fundamental achievement or development. There are other good citizens who engage zealously in world-federalism movements. Still others advocate substituting a parliamentary form of government for the one we have. A few express belief that we cannot hope certainly to endure unless we amend our Constitution so as to specify therein forms completely unifying our government, clearly subordinating the states, and eliminating any chance of claiming that national powers are divided between three "separate and equal" branches. It requires extreme optimism—or credulity—to believe any of these changes likely in the ordinary course of coming decades.

It is certainly true that our Constitution was designed to make governmental decision-making a slow and cumbersome process, maximizing give and take rather than decisiveness; and surely there are more instances now than in the days of Washington when decisions need to be made rapidly and firmly. The dominance of geographical identification and responsibility in representational patterns puts a premium on parochialism rather than on the general interest. The fact that congressional committee chairmen come to their powerful positions by mere seniority rather than by election in caucus greatly strengthens parochial attitudes. Even the relatively enlightened Supreme Court position in strengthening legislative prerogatives does this indiscriminatingly for national and state legislatures alike. In its enlightenment it minimizes the difficulties of the separation of powers, so far as the judiciary is concerned, but it does not similarly minimize the old "federal" theory.

It is certainly also true that the present structure of the government and the structure of society somehow fail to produce strong leadership except in time of crisis. *If our most pressing task is to avoid crisis, we need strong and able leadership continually.*

In sum, there is great need for new emphasis on public problems; there is great need to get abler leadership and to provide it with more assurance of co-operation between the branches of government and between the levels of government. One of the weightiest of the responsibilities of such leadership, so equipped, is to effect closer relationships between nations.

The concerns are wholly valid. Feasible solutions will be developed, however, only through responsible leadership using institutional resources. Probably, too, the needed reforms can be achieved only through a good many actions, not by some consolidated, drastic action. The very features of our government that make drastic reform seem obligatory would defeat the effort except at the height of a very great crisis, when it would almost certainly be too late.

The Congress in anything like "normal" conditions is not likely to propose to the states, or to conventions within the states, constitutional amendments which would in specific verbiage seem to weaken its own position. Similarly, the Congress would not propose specific verbiage appearing to weaken the position of the states. The states surely would not ratify the latter and almost certainly would not ratify the former proposal.

There is an extensive body of experience with efforts to modify state constitutions, and this experience points to a judgment that the more extensive and drastic the changes proposed, the more certain they are to fail of adoption. It points also to the need for successive and protracted efforts to effect even moderate changes.

In the case of the national Constitution the only amendments that might be thought to effect any change at all in the basic structural arrangements are those enacted just after the Civil War, when vindictiveness played a part and when carpet-bagger governments—or the paralyzed conditions of the conquered states in the South—were crucial to adoption. The increased power over election procedures in the states was for a long time hardly used in practice and is still exercised with extreme moderation. If possible at all, verbal amendment in pursuit of greater governmental unity would probably produce results short of actual present practice attained by interpretation and evolution.

If the amending process should be put to a new national convention, which is hardly conceivable, the results would almost certainly be retrogressive. Where are the modern Madisons, Hamiltons, Jeffersons, and Washingtons to serve in such a convention? Without the long period of incubation in political discussion which preceded the convention of 1787, even persons potentially as able as the great men who sat in that convention could not do so well. If there were such persons, it is unlikely that many of them would be made delegates. The case of France is again illustrative. One constitution after another was the product of the same type of persons, and repeated the errors which had caused the former document to fail. It was not until de Gaulle, from a different background, came to dominance in a time of crisis that reforms otherwise never attainable could be put into effect.

Citizens who may never have been disposed to think constitutional reform needed may well find concern in considering how difficult it would be to achieve it if there were need for it. And they might ponder the remark of one seasoned sage and statesman about "democracy's built-in self-destructive device." He said that the eagerness of people to be told that all is well, and the eagerness of politicians to tell them this, is a perfect prescription for inaction and ultimate failure.

The Probably Feasible

We cannot know now with certainty the needs to provide for in formal changes of constitutional language, and we would have slight hope that they might be secured. Yet gradually through the years the practices of government have been changing. By formal interpretation sometimes, by spontaneous but unconscious informal changes in interpretation at other times, by tragic civil war in one instance, we have been able to find in the document the Founders gave us a warrant for meeting our necessities. The short Constitution was undoubtedly intended to facilitate this evolutionary process.

The major problem today is to recognize this process more

clearly, to sharpen our insights to see our present necessities more realistically, and to use better the facilities already available. Some small, supplementary amendments will be attainable. The purpose of this volume has been to stimulate the pursuit of political understanding and increased skill in applying it, to the end of accelerating evolution and avoiding crises by enhancing political vitality and improving its performance.

Chief structural weaknesses are the checks and balances usually referred to as a "separation of powers in three equal branches," the attribution of a "federal system" dividing governmental sovereignty among fifty-one entities, and the exaggeration of "local egoisms" effected by these and the representational pattern. All these detract from governmental unity and limit effectiveness.

Even the structural weaknesses are in part, however, intellectual attributions. The degree of their reality depends on the persistence of old ways of thinking and speaking about the government. In practice, not least because of the Civil War, the states have become steadily more subordinate. In practice, the courts have avoided initiating jurisdiction and otherwise have exercised restraint; in so doing they have conceded increments of power to both executive and legislative branches. In practice, the Congress and the country have come to rely increasingly on executive leadership.

Experience and evolution have been carrying us in the direction we should go. With popular co-operation and understanding, the evolution can be accelerated. The first essential is to see the need and the desirable direction in which further development should go. This is to say that there should be less parroting of old dogmas and more preoccupation with present necessities. The second is to seek out and support stronger leadership and practices enlarging the supply of leadership material. This need divides into a variety of categories, involving leadership for cities, states, and the nation; for program leadership in professional and civil service ranks; and for the very rare personnel suitable for high executive posts with great political responsibilities, for party organizational posts, for legislatures, for courts, and for work with other nations.

As stated, these two requirements are the direct responsibilities of citizens, requiring only fresh thinking, closer attention to government, and more work in behalf of public affairs. There is a third category of requirements which would involve changes in statutes or in the Constitution, but few enough and free enough of consequences unwelcome to agencies essential to enactment as to appear likely in time to get official acceptance.

Citizen support would be essential to statutory changes. Those that might be considered would include model laws facilitating transfer of professional and civil service personnel from one state to another, from state to city, from city to state, from state or city to the national government, and from national government to state and city. Such interchangeability would enrich the public service generally by facilitating more nicely adjusted personnel placement than now is possible, and by breaking down one form of parochialism which now insists on employment of local persons.

With this pattern established it might become more feasible to secure similar mobility for professional executives who have reached the level of political service, having in effect given up, or never having had, civil service status. More able persons would take political posts if they were likely to be considered for similar places in other jurisdictions when there are shifts in party control. This point relates to state cabinet and deputy personnel, national "Little Cabinet," state, city, and national budget directors, deputy directors, assistants to department heads, some heads of bureaus of a newer and more novel programmatic sort, or for special reasons more involved in policy change than other bureaus, and assistants to heads of such bureaus. Public support of practices giving especially high salaries, or disproportionately large increments in retirement benefits, or both, to such persons would also make more of them available for selection when needed.

Changes in important party customs and rules governing the organization of legislative houses, while not usually statutory in the full sense of that word, are made with at least corresponding difficulty. Yet the party can be made very much more an instrument of national unity than it now is. This improvement is dependent in the first instance on citizens. When they see how policy differences are, more often than many voters realize, of the same sort at each level of government, and when they give support more consistently than now is done to the same party at all levels, they will make one of the most significant of all readily feasible governmental reforms.

At each level there will be particular steps to take in pursuit of the general reform. At the national level, for example, ways should be developed by which the president might, in an orderly, recognized, and acceptable way, have more voice in the choice of party leaders in the two houses of Congress. Committee chairmen should be elected in caucus and thus be put under obligation to the whole houses, and subject to a greater degree of control by party leaders—notably the president in the case of the party of the chief executive. There should be an end to the "senatorial courtesy" that permits a single senator to veto a presidential appointment. Finally, the parties should have more capacity for exercising discipline over recalcitrants elected or seeking election under their auspices. If the national party should be an important source of funds for state and local party organizations, capacity for discipline would be enhanced. National convention requirements and other measures guarding against organizational disloyalty of delegates to conventions, electors, and party nominees to various offices should also be provided.

These particular purposes and some others would be supported by the one constitutional amendment I am inclined to advance as evolutionary—not revolutionary—and as probably feasible in the course of a few years, if given adequate agitation and support among citizens. This would be the amendment referred to earlier in this book, and inferentially suggested by Chester Barnard in an article in the *Political Science Review* in the early 1950's.

If on national party tickets there should be with each candidate for president and vice-president, selected by the nominee for president, two candidates for senator at large, and four, or possibly five, candidates for representative at large, the consequences might be rather considerable.

Such an arrangement should be somewhat attractive to everybody, rather than objectionable. It would afford a new way to national eminence for especially outstanding legislators without taking them outside the legislative milieu. It would make them nationally responsible, and would seem likely to influence other ambitious legislators to take the national viewpoint and to adhere more consistently to positions of their party and their president. These legislators, when on the winning ticket, would usually offer means of closer association and communication with the legislative bodies.

The legislators so elected would have voting privileges within their respective houses, and presumably special influence on the choice of house leaders. Their relationship to the conventional leadership positions would be the most difficult feature of the whole arrangement. This is an aspect of the plan that requires careful handling.

Sometime the legislators may even be mature enough to establish by caucus rule the right of the national party chairman and vice-chairman to sit and vote in the caucuses of both parties. In any case, the objective behind proposals of the sort here set forth illustrate ways in which more nationally responsible performance may be developed.

As Americans mature it is their sovereign responsibility to exact higher types of leadership and to give that leadership better structures in which local egoisms yield more readily to a patriotism which, while deeper than ever, has attained a new breadth. Realization of self-interest can no longer have less than planetary perspective and implementation. But the instruments of the ablest leaders must be basically institutional. Our new professions at the world level will not be in fact reassuring except as we demonstrate that we have learned to conduct our own institutional affairs in sufficiently whole-nation terms.